THE NATIONAL EXECUTIVE BRANCH

The National Executive Branch

AN INTRODUCTION

James W. Davis, Jr.

 THE FREE PRESS NEW YORK
COLLIER-MACMILLAN LTD., LONDON

THE FREE PRESS
A Division of The Macmillan Company
866 Third Avenue, New York, New York 10022

Collier-Macmillan Canada Ltd., Toronto, Ontario

Library of Congress Catalog Card Number: 72–96834

Printing Number
1 2 3 4 5 6 7 8 9 10

CONTENTS

UNDERSTANDING THE ORGANIZATIONS   79

★★★★
★

THE EXECUTIVE BRANCH IN THE
POLITICAL SYSTEM   121

CHANGE, PROBLEM-SOLVING, AND
PROGRAM DEVELOPMENT   149

THE BUDGETING PROCESS   167

THE POLITICS OF ORGANIZATION   194

PREFACE

BOTH a textbook and an essay, this book is written primarily for college undergraduates in political science courses, though graduate students and others may find it useful. I have written it because I have not been altogether satisfied with available material that deals with the American bureaucracy. A number of brief books deal with Congress, the President, the Supreme Court, and parties and interest groups, but somehow the Executive Branch has been either ignored or mistreated. Not many brief texts dealing with the bureaucracy are available, and those that have been written often have a legalistic or principles-of-public-administration flavor. This book strives instead for a blending of public policy and political flavors. I hope that some instructors and—as important—their students will find it useful.

As I wrote the book I had in mind several political science courses. Instructors who like to use paperbacks in the common course in American politics or American government, alone or as supplements to a text, may find this book appropriate. (I hope they do use some book dealing with the Executive Branch or the bureaucracy. It is too large and important a topic to get short shrift.) This book could also be used in courses dealing primarily with the bureaucracy or the civil service and should be useful for undergraduate courses in public administration. Finally, it may be relevant to courses on the American presidency. I do not mean with these comments to limit the use of the book. Instructors are free to use their imaginations, and students may read it on their own.

What was originally a joint effort became mine alone, but I want to thank Randall Ripley for encouraging me to get started. The staff of The Free Press is due gratitude for patiently tolerating unforeseen delays. Jean and Warren have let me write the book, and Jean even found time to read it.

JAMES W. DAVIS, JR.
St. Louis, November 1969

James W. Davis, Jr. is Associate Professor of Political Science at Washington University. He has served as an advisor to the National Institute of Development Administration, in Bangkok, Thailand, and is the author of other books and journal articles in the field.

THE NATIONAL EXECUTIVE BRANCH

★

THE IMPORTANCE OF THE EXECUTIVE BRANCH

THE FIRST point to be made by a book on the Executive Branch of the United States government is that the President and the Executive Branch are not synonymous. The Executive Branch is composed of numerous organizations—departments, agencies, administrations, bureaus, services, and commissions—and millions of employees. By law, the President of the United States is Chief of the Executive Branch, but in fact he can be ignored and frustrated by employees and organizations that do not need him and will continue long after he has gone. It is sensible, therefore, to regard the Executive Branch not as an orderly hierarchy with the President on top but rather as a complex and confusing collection

Notes for this chapter appear on pages 19–20.

of organizations supervised more or less closely with more or less success by successive Presidents. This book deals primarily with the organizations and people that make up the Executive Branch, with what is frequently called the bureaucracy.

The second point to be made is that the Executive Branch is important. Its importance is frequently given lip service (and pen service) by political scientists, but they commonly go quickly on to other aspects of the American political system. Such behavior is not hard to understand. Many organizations in the Executive Branch are not as glamorous or as visible as other participants in American politics, and it may be natural to focus attention on what can be plainly seen. It is hard, however, to imagine anything more visible than the Internal Revenue Service in April, the Selective Service System when the draft notice comes, or the Post Office when the mail is late. The Executive Branch is large and diffuse, which may make study of it seem a hopeless, fruitless task. The President is one man, the Supreme Court nine, and the Congress 535. All these officials are located much of the time under a few roofs in Washington, D.C. In contrast the Executive Branch has almost 3,000,000 employees in scores of major organizations. Its units are located all around the world, as well as all over the United States.

Further, materials to study are easier to acquire if one focuses on Congress or the Court rather than on the Executive Branch. Congressional committees hold public hearings that are published, the debates of Congress appear in the Congressional Record, and roll calls are available for all to analyze. If these materials are not enough, then Congressmen can be interviewed. Judicial decisions are likewise a matter of public record. However, what goes on within the Executive Branch is not so public. Debates and decisions within the Executive

Branch are not often exposed to public view, and it is not common practice among bureaucrats to stand up and be counted. It may be too emphatic to say that Executive Branch officials have a passion for anonymity, but enough of them prefer it often enough to make research and writing about the Executive Branch difficult.

Despite these problems the Executive Branch is too important to ignore or pass over lightly. This chapter briefly summarizes the major government programs carried out by Executive Branch organizations and analyzes the various functions performed by the Executive Branch. The summary will serve merely to illustrate the number and variety of programs; many are given a sentence only and many more are not included.[1] But even this summary clearly illustrates the importance of the Executive Branch.

A Summary of Program Areas

NATIONAL DEFENSE   The Defense Department is the largest department in the Executive Branch, and the programs of the Defense Department receive the largest share of the government budget—almost half of it. Armed forces are maintained around the globe, Strategic Air Command planes and Polaris submarines are scattered around the world, and forces both in training and ready for action are maintained in this country. For the last few years much money has been spent in Vietnam. In addition a Reserve and National Guard and a conscription system are supported. To ensure that units can be moved to points where they are needed, transportation facilities must be ready. Information and orders must flow back and forth between Washington, D.C., and commands elsewhere; for this purpose a vast com-

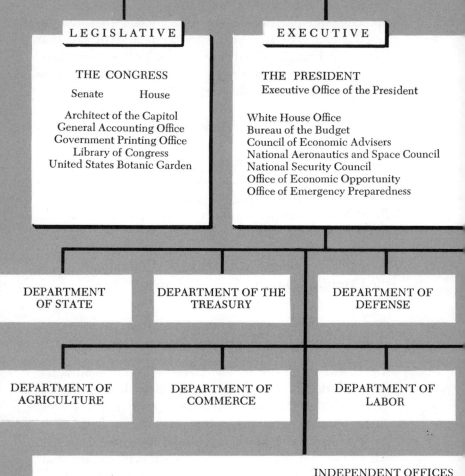

THE CONSTITUTION

LEGISLATIVE

THE CONGRESS

Senate   House

Architect of the Capitol
General Accounting Office
Government Printing Office
Library of Congress
United States Botanic Garden

EXECUTIVE

THE PRESIDENT
Executive Office of the President

White House Office
Bureau of the Budget
Council of Economic Advisers
National Aeronautics and Space Council
National Security Council
Office of Economic Opportunity
Office of Emergency Preparedness

DEPARTMENT
OF STATE

DEPARTMENT OF THE
TREASURY

DEPARTMENT OF
DEFENSE

DEPARTMENT OF
AGRICULTURE

DEPARTMENT OF
COMMERCE

DEPARTMENT OF
LABOR

INDEPENDENT OFFICES

Administrative Conference of the U.S.
Atomic Energy Commission
Civil Aeronautics Board
District of Columbia
Export-Import Bank of the U.S.
Farm Credit Administration
Federal Communications Commission
Federal Deposit Insurance Corporation
Federal Home Loan Bank Board

Federal Maritime Commission
Federal Mediation and
   Conciliation Service
Federal Power Commission
Federal Reserve System, Board of
   Governors of the
Federal Trade Commission
General Services Administration
Interstate Commerce Commission

The Government
of The United States

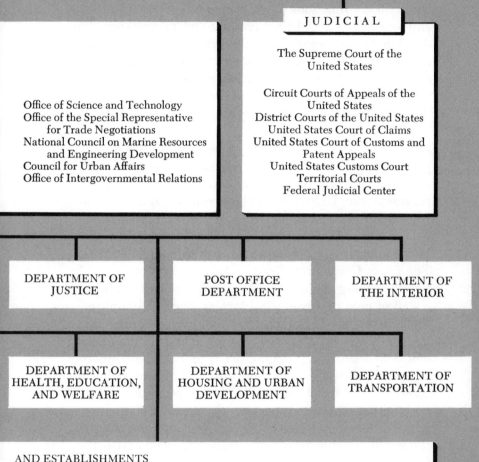

JUDICIAL

The Supreme Court of the
United States

Circuit Courts of Appeals of the
United States
District Courts of the United States
United States Court of Claims
United States Court of Customs and
Patent Appeals
United States Customs Court
Territorial Courts
Federal Judicial Center

Office of Science and Technology
Office of the Special Representative
for Trade Negotiations
National Council on Marine Resources
and Engineering Development
Council for Urban Affairs
Office of Intergovernmental Relations

DEPARTMENT OF JUSTICE	POST OFFICE DEPARTMENT	DEPARTMENT OF THE INTERIOR
DEPARTMENT OF HEALTH, EDUCATION, AND WELFARE	DEPARTMENT OF HOUSING AND URBAN DEVELOPMENT	DEPARTMENT OF TRANSPORTATION

AND ESTABLISHMENTS

National Aeronautics
and Space Administration
National Foundation on the
Arts and the Humanities
National Labor Relations Board
National Mediation Board
National Science Foundation
Railroad Retirement Board
Securities and Exchange Commission

Selective Service System
Small Business Administration
Smithsonian Institution
Tax Court of the United States
Tennessee Valley Authority
U. S. Civil Service Commission
U. S. Information Agency
U. S. Tariff Commission
Veterans Administration

Source: *United States Government Organization Manual, 1969–70.*

munications network is maintained. Numerous specialized military functions range from intelligence collection and analysis to aerial photography and mapmaking. To develop new weapons, new delivery systems, and new tactics, the Defense Department supports research and development. To supply these many units and activities, the Defense Supply Agency procures well over a billion dollars worth of material every year.

INTERNATIONAL AFFAIRS   The United States Department of State maintains embassies, missions, and consulates in practically every country of the world to represent the United States government and to assist United States citizens. The Agency for International Development (AID) administers technical assistance programs and provides loans and grants to many countries. The Peace Corps provides volunteer workers to many of the developing countries and maintains in host countries a staff of paid professionals (doctors, nurses, administrators) to assist the volunteers. In many countries the United States Information Agency (USIA) maintains offices that provide foreign citizens and resident Americans with American books, records, and movies and also sponsor a variety of cultural exchange programs. Moreover, the USIA also operates the Voice of America, which beams news and special events programs around the world. To this list of organizations can be added the Central Intelligence Agency (CIA), which has officers in many embassies and operates worldwide. All these organizations have their headquarters in Washington, and many of their activities—everything from intelligence analysis to the issuance of passports—go on there.

URBAN PROBLEMS   A variety of programs focused on the problems of the cities are administered by agencies in the Department of Housing and Urban Development (HUD). Slum clearance and urban renewal projects funded by the Renewal Assistance Administration and its predecessors have been carried out in many American cities, and public housing reflects the activity of the Housing Assistance Administration. The Federal Housing Administration insures mortgages on private family housing and on other types of shelter, such as housing for the elderly, nursing homes, and condominium housing. The Department of Housing and Urban Development through its constituent units carries out a number of other programs concerned with such things as urban planning and design and the provision of recreational space in urban areas.

PUBLIC WELFARE   Programs aimed directly at assisting individuals are administered by the Department of Health, Education, and Welfare (HEW), the Department of Labor, and the Office of Economic Opportunity. The Social Security Administration has responsibility for the old age, survivors, and disability insurance program. The Welfare Administration funds and oversees various welfare programs carried out by the welfare departments of the 50 states. The Department of Labor, and particularly the Manpower Administration within the Department of Labor, administers and develops programs designed to aid the unemployed and the underemployed. The Office of Economic Opportunity funds research on poverty, helps develop and coordinate government anti-poverty programs, and carries out programs of its own.

PUBLIC HEALTH   The Public Health Service and the National Institutes of Health are famous for their health research. The federal government also supports many other health programs. Grants are made to states and localities to help finance hospital construction. Scholarship programs are specifically designed to help students through medical school and thus increase the supply of doctors. Medicare and Medicaid provide medical services to the nation's aged and indigent men and women. The work of the Food and Drug Administration tries to protect the population from impure food and unsafe drugs, and the Water Pollution Control Administration (in the Department of the Interior) can be regarded as a health agency as well as a conservation agency.

EDUCATION   The Office of Education is the center of the education activities of the federal government; it collects a variety of statistics and carries on research intended to describe and improve American education. It also administers grant programs. Funds are available to improve teacher-training programs and a variety of school programs; construction grants are available for both academic and living facilities at colleges and universities; and Office of Education student loan programs aid needy students. The Office of Education tries to insure that its grants are used in accordance with the law. Today that means that the Office of Education has been in the forefront of the school desegregation battle.

In addition to the Office of Education, other departments are also involved in education. The Department of Labor through the Manpower Administration is involved in vocational, educational, and retraining programs; the Bureau of Indian Affairs in the Department of the Interior is engaged in American Indian education programs; and the Armed Forces are involved in a variety of educational activities.

VETERANS' AFFAIRS   The Veterans' Administration provides medical care to veterans and their dependents in veterans' hospitals, oversees the payment of disability benefits, insures loans to veterans when they buy houses, and through the famous GI bill contributes to the education of many veterans. Although these and other services are not in kind substantially different from services provided through the Department of Health, Education, and Welfare and the Department of Housing and Urban Development, the services of the Veterans' Administration are provided to a particular group of citizens, the veterans of the nation's wars.

COMMERCE AND TRANSPORTATION   This single label covers programs carried out by the Department of Commerce, the Department of Transportation, and many regulatory agencies. Highway construction has been the most costly of the activities in this area; the interstate highway system was paid for with a combination of 90 per cent federal funds and 10 per cent state funds. The Federal Highway Administration within the Department of Transportation administers the interstate highway programs as well as the other highway programs of the government. This organization also administers legislation that authorizes the federal government to specify safety and performance standards for automobiles. The Federal Aviation Administration within the Department of Transportation controls all commercial air traffic and oversees air safety. This latter concern is shared with the Civil Aeronautics Board, a body which controls the routes and rates of commercial airlines. A number of other regulatory agencies (including the Interstate Commerce Commission, the Federal Communications Commission, and the Federal Trade Commission) oversee the services provided and the rates charged by major industries in different sectors of the nation's economy. The United States Coast Guard is to some degree part of the defense establishment and in time of war is under the jurisdiction of the Defense Department; but it is charged with enforcing many regulations covering water safety at all times for all citizens.

The data collected and analyzed by the Census Bureau and the research conducted by the National Bureau of Standards (both in the Department of Commerce) are used by business and industry as well as a variety of other consumers. The Environmental Science Services Administration provides information ranging from weather reports to coastal charts to business and industry as well as to individual citizens. The patent system administered by the Patent Office protects large corporations as well as individual inventors.

AGRICULTURE AND NATURAL RESOURCES   Programs designed to stabilize farm family income, to finance rural housing, and to finance rural electrification and telephone service are carried on by units of the Department of Agriculture. Many of the programs administered by this department are not unlike those administered in HEW and HUD, but they are directed to people in rural areas.

In the face of a rapidly growing world population and a food shortage in much of the world, agricultural research receives particular attention from the Department of Agriculture. Human nutrition, plant and animal diseases, and increased crop yields are all subjects of inquiry. Both the Department of Agriculture and the Department of the Interior carry out programs intended to conserve the natural resources of the country and to provide recreational space to the public. The Soil Conservation Service is concerned, as its name suggests, with watershed protection and flood control. The Forest Service manages 187,000,000 acres of National Forests, and the National Park Service has responsibility for almost 14,000,000 acres of National Parks as well as other parks and monuments. The Bureau of Land Management manages government lands not designated as National Forests, National Parks, or military reservations. Other organizations in this area are the Bureau of Mines, the Bureau of Reclamation, the Bureau of Sport Fisheries and Wildlife, and the Bureau of Outdoor Recreation.

RESEARCH AND DEVELOPMENT   Research and development have been mentioned several times; research is an important component of many government activities. Earth orbiting, moon orbiting, and moon landings are the most dramatic and visible of the projects carried out by the National Aeronautics and Space Administration; but weather, communications, and reconnaissance satellites all owe their existence to the space research activities backed by the government. The Atomic Energy Commission supports research on both military and peacetime applications of atomic energy, and the National Science Foundation provides funds to academic institutions and scientists for research on a wide variety of topics.

GENERAL GOVERNMENT   In addition to the many activities mentioned above there must inevitably be a category of miscellany. This group includes the Post Office Department, whose functions are known to everyone. Units of the Treasury Department collect taxes, write checks, manage the debt, guard the White House, and protect the President. The Bureau of Immigration and Naturalization, the Federal Bureau of Investigation, and the Bureau of Prisons are components of the Department of Justice. Moreover, a host of independent agencies ranging from the Civil Service Commission and

General Services Administration to the Battle Monuments Commission can be placed in the general government category.

A CAUTIONARY NOTE   The Executive Branch as a whole does very little; programs are carried out by specific organizations, though of course major problems (poverty, civil rights) may involve many organizations. Throughout the rest of this book it will pay to remember that the Executive Branch is made up of a number of organizations doing different things, often for different people. The result is that particular organizations may be independent of the President or dependent on him; they may be influential or without influence, praised or criticized, successful or failing, flourishing or withering, efficient or profligate. Which adjectives apply to a particular organization depends on what it is doing how well for whom.

The Functions of the Executive Branch

So far we have seen that at least some of the programs carried out in the Executive Branch are immensely significant for the security and well-being of the population. But even these familiar observations are enough to suggest the importance of individual Executive Branch organizations and the importance of the Executive Branch as a whole. Although it may be too much to say that the Executive Branch is the government, the facts point in that direction. Some years ago the distinguished political scientist Carl Friedrich observed[2] that bureaucracy was the core of modern government; today the Executive Branch appears to be the dominant branch of the American government. Today is the Age of the Executive.

It is important to understand that Executive Branch organizations are frequently heavily involved in the planning and development of their own programs. To be sure, the popular image of American government is otherwise. The myth says that legislation authorizing programs comes from Congress and is simply implemented by executive agencies. A somewhat more accurate version is that the President proposes; the Congress reviews, perhaps modifies, and authorizes; and executive agencies implement. But in fact much program legislation is initiated by the agencies themselves,[3] reviewed by the Office of Legislative Reference in the Bureau of the Budget, goes to Congress where it is considered and acted on, and after approval by the President returns for implementation to the agency that initiated it. Program development and implementation is a more circular process than is commonly thought, and Congress may be not much more than a weighing station.

In a recent essay Samuel Huntington wrote that in the nineteenth century Congress "frequently took the legislative initiative in dealing with major national problems."[4] He thinks that this no longer holds true. "Today's aggressive spirit is clearly the executive branch."[5] According to Huntington, Congress has lost not only the initiative, but also its former dominant influence on the content of final legislation. Congress may delay and modify, but the major power is the Executive Branch.

Of course, within the Executive Branch much power belongs to the President; but his time, his interests, and his information are all limited. The political executives and senior civil servants in the Executive Branch organizations are in the end responsible for developing and modifying the programs carried out by the organizations. What they fail to do may not get done; what they do not suggest, may not be suggested. They are, after all, the only ones giving continuing attention to a particular organization and its set of problems and programs.

In their standard text on public administration John Pfiffner and Robert Presthus point out that over half the legislation considered by the Congress originates in Executive Branch agencies.[6] If we delete from consideration all the private bills that Congress takes up and consider only major legislation, then the proportion of Executive-initiated bills would be even higher. Not only political scientists point to the importance of the Executive Branch. The political columnist Richard Rovere has written: "During most of this century, most advocates of social change of any broad and consequential kind have felt that the federal government, and especially its executive branch, is the only really effective agency of change."[7] In the same vein the sociologist Peter Blau has observed: "In the large and complex society of today the implementation of new social policies requires bureaucratic machinery."[8]

These several observations can be easily summed up. Where is much legislation initiated and drafted? In the Executive Branch. Where is it implemented? In the Executive Branch. Legislation as it comes from Congress is interpreted, enlarged, enforced, or ignored. Executive Branch organizations spend most of the budget (one agency alone collects most of the revenue), and the employees of Executive Branch organizations deal directly with the public.

There are other ways of describing the roles, activities, and functions of Executive Branch organizations. We can ask what is included in program initiation and program implementation. Program initiation includes such activities as data collection and analysis (search or intelligence activity), problem formulation, program design, legislative bill drafting, and program selling or lobbying. Program implementation may include such activities as organization or reorganization, resource acquisition and allocation, staffing and training, rule development and enforcement, and public education. Naming these activities makes clearer still the breadth and significance of Executive Branch functions.

A more general approach to an understanding of the importance of the Executive Branch is an inquiry into its functioning in the political system. Gabriel Almond and G. Bingham Powell have carried out just such an inquiry; their observations are worth attention. They begin by giving meaning to the term *political system;* they discuss inputs (demands and supports) and outputs (such as taxes, regulations, and services) and suggest six functions that are performed in a political system.[9]

1. Demands are formulated (interest articulation).
2. Demands are combined in the form of alternative courses of action (interest aggregation).
3. Authoritative rules are formulated (rule making).
4. These rules are applied and enforced (rule application).
5. These applications of rules are adjudicated in individual cases (rule adjudication).
6. These various activities are communicated both within the political system and between the political system and its environment (communication).

Which of these functions are performed by Executive Branch organizations? The short answer is, "all of them." Obviously men in the Executive Branch apply or enforce laws, rules, orders, and decisions. This is so clear that Almond and Powell say,[10] "We would like to argue the thesis that bureaucracies tend to monopolize outputs." They elaborate:[11]

In addition to having this monopoly of rule enforcement, bureaucracies are typically of great importance
in the processes of rule making. In the modern era
most legislation is of a very general kind; in order that
it may be effectively enforced, administrative officials
must work out regulations or regulatory codes elab-
orating the policy which has been adopted by the
political branches of the government. Usually the extent to which a general policy is carried out is dependent upon the interpretations which bureaucrats give
to it, and upon the spirit and the will of bureaucrats.
In addition we know that a great deal of the adjudication carried on by modern political systems is carried
on not by independent courts, but by administrative
agencies, whether they be organized as independent
regulatory bodies or as units in regular operating departments.

Almond and Powell also point out that Executive
Branch organizations may be articulators and aggre-
gators of interest:[12]

Finally, bureaucracies are of enormous importance in
the communication function in political systems. Even
in democratic political systems, the bureaucracy is one
of the most important sources, if not the most important source, of information about public issues and
politically significant events. Newspapermen and radio
and television newscasters are constantly knocking at
the doors of administrative officials in search of the
latest information in all spheres of foreign and domestic policy. While an aggressive press in a modern
democratic society has considerable leverage in forcing
information out of the bureaucracy, it is quite clear
that bureaucrats have some control over the amount
of information which is transmitted and the way in
which it is interpreted. The decisions made by political elites, whether they be executives or legislators, are

also based in considerable part on the kind of information which they are able to get from administrative agencies. Similarly, interest groups, political parties, and the public are dependent on information transmitted by administrative officials.

A consequence of the Executive Branch's many functions is that other participants in the political system must often work through it and depend on it to get what they want. But this point, once made, must be qualified. We have seen already and will see again the many different organizations in the Executive Branch. Not all of them perform these several functions equally actively or equally well. Although it is convenient to speak of "the Executive Branch" or "the bureaucracy," it is important to remember that this branch of government is not a pod filled with similar peas. It is more like a basket filled with mixed fruit—ranging in size from berries to melons and in condition from green to overripe.

No reasons for the Executive Branch's involvement in so many functions have been offered so far, but several can be given. One reason is simply the great expansion of government activity in the twentieth century, especially since the Depression and World War II. Congress has in effect coped with its workload by delegating many jobs to agencies of the Executive Branch. Administrative agencies today devise rules to implement legislation passed in very general form by Congressmen not equipped and without time to legislate details. In addition, the judicial role of administrative agencies has been expanded by Congress. When the courts cannot cope with their work load, Congress has two obvious alternatives. One is to increase the number of courts, and this step has been taken. Another is to give administrative agencies judicial authority to hear certain types of cases, and this step has also been taken. Part of the job of the independent regulatory agencies (and other agencies as well) is to hold hearings and make judgments.

In explaining the importance of the Executive Branch today it is also important to recognize that problems confronted by the government are often soluble only with information and techniques possessed by men in the Executive Branch, not by men in Congress or on the bench. The Executive Branch is ideally the home of the expert, the specialist, the professional. It is in the Executive Branch where there are presumably men who can bring specific knowledge to bear on specific problems and program design.

Two other factors have enhanced the importance and influence of some Executive Branch organizations: the frequent need, particularly in national security matters, for secrecy and for speedy decision and action. Neither Congress or the Courts are well adapted to secret or quick operations. Congress by design is a deliberate body; it is characterized by intermittent sessions, open committee hearings, and open debate. None of these is consistent with either secrecy or speed. As the need for such operation (and perhaps its acceptance) has become more common in governmental matters, Executive Branch organizations have grown in consequence.

The Intent of the Book

The size and significance of the Executive Branch in this century has been a cause for concern to many observers. Popular speakers are likely to decry the burgeoning bureaucracy and to attack the decisions and ability of far-off bureaucrats. More serious students ask how to control the bureaucracy, how to keep it responsible and responsive, and they search for checks and alternatives. The chapters that follow, however, do not attack nor do they call for reform. This book tries to be simply descriptive and analytical; its intent is not to frighten but to inform. This being said, it must be said also that within the Executive Branch there is much to criticize, much that needs changing. Perhaps this book, by providing information on the structure and processes of the Executive Branch, will permit the reader to inquire and criticize more ably and to suggest changes that may be both appropriate and feasible. At the least, it should help him separate intelligent criticism of particular organizations within the Executive Branch from uninformed attacks on bureaucracy and bureaucrats.

Notes for Chapter 1

1. Detailed information on any particular organization in the Executive Branch can be found in the current *United States Government Organization Manual* and the current *United States Budget*. Congressional hearings and annual agency reports are also useful sources.

2. Carl J. Friedrich, *Constitutional Government and Democracy* (Boston: Ginn and Co., 1950), p. 37.

3. For illustrations see James W. Davis and Randall B. Ripley, "The Bureau of the Budget and Executive Branch Agencies: Notes on Their Interaction," *Journal of Politics* (1967), p. 751. "The more that an agency relies on legislation for its growth, the more it must rely on the Bureau of the Budget for support for its legislative ideas. One of the respondents in an operating agency said, 'This is a legislating agency. We go to the legislative trough constantly. We are thus involved with the Bureau of the Budget constantly.' A respondent in another agency said, 'Legislation is the area in which I get in touch with the Bureau of the Budget. We have 200 or 300 bills a year which apply to us.' Another agency respondent indicated the frequency of his contact with the Bureau: 'I have several contacts a day with the Bureau of the Budget on program matters. Under the law we develop a work program and then must go to the Congress through the President, which means the Bureau of the Budget.' "

4. Samuel P. Huntington, "Congressional Responses to the Twentieth Century," in David B. Truman (ed.), *The Congress and America's Future* (Englewood Cliffs, N.J.: Prentice-Hall, Inc., 1965), p. 23.

5. *Ibid.*

6. John M. Pfiffner and Robert Presthus, *Public Administration* (New York: The Ronald Press, 1967, 5th edition), p. 51.

7. Richard Rovere, "Letter from Washington," *New Yorker*, August 19, 1967, p. 92.

8. Peter Blau, *Bureaucracy in Modern Society* (New York: Random House, 1956), p. 91.

9. Gabriel A. Almond and G. Bingham Powell, Jr., *Comparative Politics* (Boston: Little, Brown and Co., 1966), pp. 25–29.

10. *Ibid.*, p. 153.

11. *Ibid.*, p. 154.

12. *Ibid.*, p. 155.

★★

THE ORGANIZATIONS OF THE EXECUTIVE BRANCH

ONE MAY classify Executive Branch organizations by their program responsibilities—defense, foreign affairs, human resources, and so on. Executive Branch organizations may also be classified in terms of their position within the Executive Branch or in terms of their proximity to the President. Some organizations are part of the Executive Office of the President, others are departments headed by members of the President's Cabinet, some are major independent agencies, and some are relatively obscure bureaus within departments. This chapter describes these types of organizations.

Notes for this chapter appear on pages 42–44.

The Executive Office of the President

Because the Executive Office is organizationally closest to the President and stands at the pinnacle of the Executive Branch, it seems appropriate to start this chapter by describing it. The Executive Office is relatively new; it was created in 1939 by Reorganization Order Number 1 in order to draw together (and to provide) advisors and assistants to the President.

One of the most important of the several organizations comprising the Executive Office is the White House Office. The men in this office are personal appointees of the President and serve as his personal assistants. They maintain contact with Cabinet members, sub-Cabinet officials, bureau chiefs, Congressional leaders and other Congressmen, party leaders, and interest group spokesmen. They gather information, communicate the President's wishes, and issue his orders. Members of the White House Office listen, read, speak, decide, and act for the President. The Office staff numbers close to 300, but the President may have no more than 12 or 15 special assistants. Customarily included are a press secretary, a special counsel, and an appointments secretary. Other members of the staff may specialize in particular functional or problem areas. There may be specialists in foreign affairs and defense, in welfare and education, in urban problems, and in agriculture. Usually some members of the staff are in charge of liaison with Congress. The precise organization of the White House Office and the use to which it is put differ with each President.

The largest organization in the Executive Office is the United States Bureau of the Budget.[1] Created in

1921 as a Treasury Department bureau, its purpose was to assist the President in the preparation of the United States Budget. In 1937 the President's Committee on Administrative Management recommended that it be transferred from the Treasury, and in 1939 it was made a part of the Executive Office of the President. The Bureau of the Budget is headed by a director who, like members of the White House Office, is a personal appointee of the President; he is not subject to Senate confirmation. Several of his immediate assistants are also appointed, either by the President or by the director, but the bulk of the Bureau staff is made up of career civil servants. The Bureau uses about 300 professional employees in its various offices and divisions, as well as a clerical force.

The Bureau of the Budget was created, as its name suggests, to prepare and execute the budget of the United States. It is still engaged in this business, but today it is involved as well in everything from fiscal policy to management improvement to program evaluation. The full extent of its activity changes with administrations, but under recent administrations it has been quite active. In recent years the Bureau has stressed the importance of evaluating programs in terms of their costs and benefits, and it has strongly encouraged agencies to plan their programs. The Bureau of the Budget reviews all legislative requests from Executive Branch organizations before they go to Congress and determines whether they are in accord with the program of the President. Legislation passed by Congress is also reviewed in the Bureau before it is signed by the President, and Bureau staff members are likely to recommend that he veto any legislation that appears to weaken the power of the President. Problems of government organization and reorganization are handled within the

Bureau; even the statistical programs of the government are coordinated within the Bureau. To all these fairly well defined roles can be added the functions of Presidential troubleshooter, overseer, and fact-gatherer. The budget examiner in the Budget Bureau wears many hats and is an important link between the Chief Executive and the White House and operating agencies of the Executive Branch.

In addition to the White House Office and the Bureau of the Budget, the Executive Office contains a number of other organizations: The Council of Economic Advisors, the National Security Council, and the Office of Science and Technology are perhaps the most important and the most visible. (Until the advent of the Nixon administration the Office of Economic Opportunity (OEO) could have been included in this list.) These offices, like the White House Office and the Bureau of the Budget, combine in varying quantities advisory, supervisory, and coordinating functions. They advise the President, they supervise other units in the Executive Branch, and they try to coordinate similar work being done by a number of organizations.

The Council of Economic Advisors, created by the Employment Act of 1946, is composed of three men appointed by the President with the advice and consent of the Senate.[2] The main responsibilities of the Council are to advise the President on economic matters and to prepare an annual economic report analyzing economic developments and trends and making economic policy recommendations. The Council is concerned with a variety of economic matters including government spending, production and employment, costs, prices and profits, agriculture, state and local expenditures, and the international economy. The Council does not, however, engage in economic analysis only. A few sentences from the "Report to the President on the Activities of the Council of Economic Advisors During 1966" make this clear.

> In addition to its regular and informal consultations with other Government agencies, the Council and its staff in 1966 participated with other agencies in a large variety of more formal committees, task forces, and studies.
>
> • • •
>
> The Council and its staff represent the United States in a number of important international conferences.
>
> • • •
>
> An important responsibility of the Council is to explain and clarify the Administration's economic policies, both within the Government and to the public at large. This is done through numerous speeches, articles, press briefings, statements, Congressional testimony, its Annual Report, and by assisting the President in the preparation of his Economic Report. The Council meets frequently and informally with many visiting scholars, officials of foreign countries, men and women from the press corps, businessmen, labor leaders, State officials, bankers, and interested private citizens, and more formally with a number of advisory groups, including the President's Advisory Committee on Labor-Management Policy and the Business Council's Liaison Committee with the Council of Economic Advisors.[3]

These statements make clear that anyone interested in policy politics, as differentiated from electoral politics or party politics, must attend to the views and activities of professionals within the Executive Branch. The men who make up the Council of Economic Advisors are not politicians; they are professional economists, experts.

But in pressing for particular policies and making their views known to a wide variety of people they are surely engaging in policy politics.

The National Security Council was established in 1947 "to advise the President with respect to the integration of domestic, foreign, and military policies relating to the national security so as to enable the military services and the other departments and agencies of the Government to cooperate more effectively in matters involving the national security."[4] In effect the National Security Council is a high level interdepartmental committee with a small permanent staff. The membership includes the President, the Vice President, the Secretary of State, the Secretary of Defense, the director of the Office of Emergency Planning, and other officers when appointed by the President. Meetings of the Council are customarily also attended by the director of the Bureau of the Budget, the Secretary of the Treasury, the director of the Central Intelligence Agency, and the chairman of the Joint Chiefs of Staff. The National Security Council has no operational responsibilities but exists to consider problems of interest jointly to the several agencies concerned with national security.

When considering the functions of the National Security Council, as indeed when considering the functions of any of the units of the Executive Office of the President, it is important to remember that the precise functioning may vary noticeably from President to President. Under President Eisenhower the National Security Council was quite active and played a visible and important part in national security policy deliberations. President Kennedy and President Johnson relied on the National Security Council much less often and called meetings less frequently.[5] In the administration of President Nixon, however, it appears that the National Security Council will emerge from relative obscurity and assume something like its Eisenhower era role.

The Office of Science and Technology is yet another unit of the Executive Office of the President. Established in 1962 its main purpose is to provide scientific advice to the President and his staff. Its director in 1963, Dr. Jerome Wiesner, who was also Special Assistant to the President for Science and Technology, provided the following description of its functions to a Congressional investigating committee.

> The Office of Science and Technology was established last year to assist the President in scientific and technical policy matters and to facilitate interagency coordination, developing into a staff mechanism to serve the Special Assistant [to the President for Science and Technology], the PSAC [President's Science Advisory Committee], and the Federal Council [of Science and Technology]. Slightly more than a dozen highly trained specialists in science, engineering, and administration provide assistance to these activities—identifying issues, phrasing questions, gathering information from the agencies on problems in scientific fields, working closely with the Bureau of the Budget in the formulation and review of Federal budgets, the Council of Economic Advisers, and other Executive Office agencies; and following up on its own the implementation of Federal programs. In addition, the Office has served as the channel by which the executive branch meets its responsibilities to the Congress on matters of overall science policy.[6]

The Office of Economic Opportunity was created in 1964 as part of the Economic Opportunity Act. It was intended to coordinate existing antipoverty programs carried on by the Department of Health, Education, and Welfare, by the Department of Labor, and by the Department of Housing and Urban Development (called the Housing and Home Finance Agency when O.E.O. was created). Its coordinating role was the major justification for the location of the O.E.O. in the Executive Office. In addition, of course, locating this office within the Executive Office focused attention on the antipoverty activities of the government and gave the impression that poverty was something the President was *really* interested in. The location of such an organization, and indeed its creation, may be intended to demonstrate Presidential interest and intent. Changes in structure may be a way of signaling changes in program and policy. In addition to having a supervisory and coordinating role, the Office of Economic Opportunity, unlike other Executive Branch units, developed and carried out several programs of its own. Responsibility for many of these has now been transferred to other agencies; i.e., the Job Corps has been moved to the Department of Labor. And as this is written O.E.O. is in a state of flux.

The Cabinet Departments

In the Executive Branch there are twelve organizations that are called cabinet departments. These departments, together with their constituent units, carry out most of the programs of the federal government, spend most of the money, and employ most of the people. The major characteristic that the departments have in common and share with no other organization is that each is headed by a Presidential appointee who is a member of the President's Cabinet. Other organizations have heads appointed by the President, but they are not members of his Cabinet. But here any similarity between the departments ends. As Table 2–1 shows, the Defense

TABLE 2–1 Cabinet Departments: Their Budgets and Employees

Department	Number of Employees—1968	Budget Outlay 1969 estimate
Agriculture	108,318	7,167,000,000
Commerce	35,453	853,000,000
Defense	1,267,152	78,000,000,000
Health, Education & Welfare	107,805	45,769,000,000
Housing and Urban Development	14,559	3,216,000,000
Interior	69,417	923,000,000
Justice	33,653	555,000,000
Labor	9,882	3,800,000,000
Post Office	715,970	767,000,000
State	47,429	439,000,000
Transportation	57,929	6,282,000,000
Treasury	92,431	15,425,000,000

SOURCE: *Statistical Abstract of the United States, 1968. See Tables 541 and 569.*

Department is at one extreme in size and the Department of Labor is at the other. The budgets of the Defense Department and the State Department differ greatly. The departments also differ in age. The Department of Transportation, created in 1967, is just getting started. The Department of State is as old as the United States. The departments perform different functions, serve different interests, and have different sources of support. Some departments are more or less single-purpose organizations: The Post Office Department and the Justice Department are examples. Others are clearly conglomerates. The Department of Commerce, for example, includes the following organizations, according to the 1967–68 *United States Government Organization Manual:*

Business and Defense Services Administration
Economic Development Administration
Environmental Science Services Administration
Maritime Administration
Office of Business Economics
Office of Field Services
Office of Foreign Commercial Services
Patent Office
Office of State Technical Services
Bureau of the Census
Bureau of International Commerce
National Bureau of Standards
United States Travel Service

Given the differences among departments it is impossible to say much about organization that applies
equally to all departments, but some general statements
are possible. To assist him in the management of his
department, every Secretary has a staff composed of both
political appointees and career civil servants. Usually
a Secretary's deputy or under-secretary and several assistant secretaries are political appointees and have overall responsibility for some particular function or program
area. In the Department of Health, Education and Welfare, for example, assistant secretaries are responsible
for the following areas: Health and Scientific Affairs,
Education, Individual and Family Services, Legislation,
and Program Coordination. In addition there is an Assistant Secretary for Administration and an Assistant
Secretary, Comptroller. Each area also has deputy
assistant secretaries and special assistants. At the departmental level also can be found career civil servants who
staff the administrative structure—the budget office, personnel office, and so on—and who provide assistance

(and sometimes no doubt resistance) to the political appointees.

Below department level are the constituent organizations of a department; all departments are made up of these constituent units. There is no universally applicable terminology to describe and classify these subdepartmental units, but there are some generally used terms.

"Administration" is the term often used to describe a major unit within a department. An "Administration" may be headed either by an assistant secretary or simply by an administrator. In the Department of Labor the Manpower Administration is headed by a man who is titled "Assistant Secretary for Manpower and Manpower Administrator." The Social Security Administration is headed simply by an administrator, and the same is true of the Environmental Sciences Service Administration.

In addition to "Administrations," departments commonly have bureaus which may also be constituent units of administrations. In a sense the bureaus are the blocks with which departments are built. The word "bureaucracy" is related to the word bureau; the bureau is the basic work unit of the bureaucracy or the Executive Branch. Departments vary in the number and variety of their bureaus, and within many departments there are organizations with the position or status of a bureau, but without the name. The Justice Department houses the Federal Bureau of Investigation and the Bureau of Prisons, but the Immigration and Naturalization Service. The Department of the Interior claims the Bureau of Indian Affairs and the Bureau of Mines, but the Geological Survey. Such anomalies can often be traced to a prior independent existence of an organization whose name was not changed when it was brought into a department.

Bureaus, like departments, differ substantially in their size and organization. The United States Forest Service (Department of Agriculture) has a substantial field organization, thanks to the number of national forests. The National Park Service (Department of the Interior) sends its men in broad-brimmed hats wherever there are Parks or National Monuments. The FBI, the Secret Service, and the Internal Revenue Service all maintain field operations. The National Bureau of Standards, on the other hand, is located almost entirely in and around Washington, and the Patent Office is under one roof. Some bureaus are headed by political appointees who come and go with the President, if not more often; whereas directors of other bureaus (the FBI is a famous example) are as permanent as members of the career civil service. At least, all bureaus are located within departments and, on paper, are subordinate to cabinet secretaries and often to assistant secretaries as well.

In addition to administrations and bureaus, a variety of other organizations may be attached to departments in one way or another. The Agency for International Development is part of the State Department, but in the past it was independent and even now is semi-autonomous. The National Security Agency, according to the official statement in the *Government Organization Manual*, was begun in 1952 "as a separately organized agency within the Department of Defense." The military departments within the Department of Defense are simply noncabinet departments, whatever that may mean. Other apparent oddities could be pointed to with little trouble. It is possible to talk about principles of organization, but it is hard to find them in practice.

The Independent Agencies

About forty-five agencies in the Executive Branch are not located within departments. These independent agencies perform some of the government's most important functions and provide some of the most important services. The Civil Service Commission, the Veterans' Administration, the General Services Administration, the Atomic Energy Commission, the National Aeronautics and Space Administration, and the United States Information Agency are all examples. To be sure, some less well-known organizations are also included in the list of independent agencies: The Delaware River Basin Commission, the American Battle Monuments Commission, the Indian Claims Commission, and the Panama Canal Company may all serve as examples.

The many independent agencies are quite varied. Several are single-purpose organizations headed by a single individual. Seven are regulatory commissions. Some government corporations are also independent agencies, and a fourth category includes what can be called central service and control agencies.

Among the single-purpose agencies headed by a single individual are some of the better known of the independent agencies: NASA, the Veterans' Administration, the Selective Service System, and the United States Information Agency, for instance. Some are as big as departments; the Veterans' Administration is bigger than the Department of Labor, and the budget of NASA has been most impressive. Like departments, most of the independent agencies with a single head are organized along hierarchical lines, but an independent agency is unlikely to present the conglomerate appearance of some departments. The critical difference between independent agencies and departments, of course, is that only departments are headed by a cabinet member.

The independent regulatory agencies are as follows:

Civil Aeronautics Board (CAB)
Federal Communications Commission (FCC)
Federal Maritime Commission (FMC)
Federal Power Commission (FPC)
Federal Trade Commission (FTC)
Interstate Commerce Commission (ICC)
Securities and Exchange Commission (SEC)

These agencies have two characteristics that set them apart from other government organizations.[7] First, they are headed not by a single commissioner or director or chief, but by a multimember commission. Second, the commissioners serve for fixed terms, rather than at the pleasure of the President. A President who serves two terms may have substantial impact on a regulatory agency through his appointments, but he cannot have the immediate impact that he may have on other agencies. This impact is also tempered by the requirement that he balance his appointments. He cannot appoint only members of his own party to regulatory commissions, they must be bipartisan. Many independent agencies are independent only in that they are not part of departments, but the regulatory agencies are independent in that they are insulated from some kinds of direct Presidential influence. Congress views the regulatory agencies within its sphere of influence and has tried solicitously to protect the commissions from Presidential dominance.

Several justifications have been suggested for the independence of the regulatory agencies, all related to what these agencies do. These agencies are charged with making and enforcing rules regulating the behavior of major industries. The Interstate Commerce Commission has to decide which railroads can run to what points, whether a railroad can cancel a particular train, and what charges railroads may levy. The Civil Aeronautics Board has similar responsibilities with regard to airlines. The Federal Communications Commission controls the issuance of radio and television licenses. The Federal Trade Commission is concerned with the propriety and accuracy of advertising, among other things. Because in carrying out such responsibilities the regulatory agencies make rules (legislate) and conduct semi-judicial hearings, it may be argued, to justify their independence, that they do not belong entirely to any one branch of the government. This argument is not particularly strong, in that many departments and bureaus also perform legislative and judicial functions.

Another explanation for the independence given the regulatory agencies is that similar regulatory functions were first performed in the states by multimembered commissions. Congress used this state experience as a model when creating the Interstate Commerce Commission in 1887, and other commissions were then formed using the ICC as a model. Another reason for the independence of the agencies may be that Congress thought their functions too important to be left to the President alone.

Finally, and perhaps this is as good a reason as any, once regulation appeared inevitable, industries apparently preferred to be regulated by a specialized and relatively independent agency that they might be able to control. As it has worked out, the regulatory agencies have developed close relationships with the industries over which they have jurisdiction. The clearest example of this may be the close and supportive relationship that exists between the ICC and the railroad industry, though certainly the relationship between the FCC and the broadcasting industry has not been noted for distance or coolness.

About twenty of the organizations that make up the Executive Branch are government corporations.[8] The Tennessee Valley Authority is the best known example, but the Federal Deposit Insurance Corporation, the Federal Home Loan Bank Board, and even the Panama Canal Company also illustrate this kind of organization. The government corporations provide services that are quasi-commercial in character, and in their structure and powers they bear some resemblance to business corporations. They have more flexibility in their operations than government departments, bureaus, or other independent agencies, and their relations with the President and Congress are marked by an absence of many routine controls.

> A department must apply elaborate procedures in estimating its future financial needs and in obtaining appropriations from Congress. It enjoys no assurance of continuity in its programs, for once a year it must seek funds from a Congress that is sometimes friendly and sometimes inexplicably capricious. It must hire its employees subject to intricate procedures and regulations fixed by the Civil Service Commission. In spending money it must take care lest it violate the voluminous jurisprudence on the subject created in the decisions and interpretations of the Comptroller General.[9]

A government corporation has none of these departmental restrictions. Most important, the government corporations enjoy substantial financial flexibility. They are not subject to annual appropriations, and their earnings may be retained by them and poured directly back into their operations. Thus they do not every year have to ask the Bureau of the Budget, the President, and the Congress for funds.

Though government corporations are not subject to the usual financial restraints or controls, they are not uncontrolled. The provisions of the Government Corporation Control Act of 1945 ensure that government corporations are not free to do just as they please. Rather they are controlled in unique ways. Congress originally must authorize the corporate form of organization and specify what the corporation may and may not do. Congress may dissolve corporations. By legislation Congress may modify the authority or responsibilities of a corporation. Congress may or may not provide working capital to a corporation as it chooses. The operations of the corporations are reviewed annually by the President, the Bureau of the Budget, and the Congress. Government corporations must submit budget programs annually, though these are more like work plans than requests for funds. Because the corporation is not requesting funds, the Congress need not appropriate funds; but it must authorize expenditure from corporate funds.

Some departments include corporations that can be controlled in some measure by the department secretary. Certainly their status is different from that of ordinary bureaus, but they cannot act totally contrary to departmental policy.

Why do government corporations exist? Why is this form of organization used? The most important explanations are the need for freedom and the need for speed. As V. O. Key has suggested, the corporation is most commonly used during emergencies when speed is essential and the usual government restraints on action may hinder the response to a problem. "The major objective in the creation of most government corporations has been to carry out, under emergency conditions, functions of a commercial nature clothed with a public concern."[10] Key has noted also that when an emergency is over the corporation created to act in it often disappears. Many depression and war-born corporations have disappeared, the Reconstruction Finance Corporation and the Defense Plant Corporation among them; but the Federal Deposit Insurance Corporation and the Federal Savings and Loan Insurance Corporation, also depression born, have continued. During World War II there were a hundred corporations, today there are only twenty. Generally, the number of government corporations in existence depends on the demands the government faces.

Three executive agencies might properly be called central service and control agencies: the Bureau of the Budget, the Civil Service Commission, and the General Services Administration (GSA). The Bureau of the Budget has already been discussed as a unit of the Executive Office, however; so these paragraphs will describe the Civil Service Commission and the GSA. These two organizations differ substantially in organization as well as in mission, but they are alike in that they provide service primarily to other government agencies rather than to the public and control other government agencies, rather than industries or members of the public.

The United States Civil Service Commission was created in 1883 to administer a personnel merit system for the federal government. The Commission is composed of three members appointed by the President. Reorganization Plan 5 of 1949 provided for the designation of a chairman and vice chairman by the President.

The chairman is the chief executive officer of the Civil Service Commission, and since 1949 the commission has in some respects resembled an independent agency with a single administrator. The other two commissioners take part in some policy decisions and also have appellate functions, but they take little part in the day-to-day functioning of the U.S. Civil Service Commission.

O. Glenn Stahl has provided in his text on *Public Personnel Administration* a useful description of the current role and operations of the Commission.[11]

> The United States Civil Service Commission is by all odds the largest and most highly organized central personnel establishment in modern government, embracing a number of regional and subsidiary offices servicing federal installation scattered throughout the country and abroad and superintending between 800 and 900 decentralized boards of examiners manned by experts in the operating departments. Its functions cover recruitment, examining, job evaluation, training, and the administration of personnel investigations and retirement and insurance systems. Its principal role in most of these functions is that of policy making and standard setting for the decentralized personnel activities of the agencies and inspection for adequacy of agency personnel administration.

From Stahl's description of both the service and the control functions of the Commission, it is clear that the Commission deals almost solely with other government agencies. Thanks to the increasing number of employees in the career civil service and to the increasing range of Commission activities, Herbert Kaufman has said that the Civil Service Commission is the "kingpin of federal personnel administration."[12]

> Formally, the personnel function was widely scattered. The basic framework was provided by legislation and

by executive orders of the President issued under authority conferred on him by statute and by the Constitution directly. More detailed regulations were issued by the Civil Service Commission, whose staff then either executed the provisions of the regulations or exercised surveillance over the line agencies to ensure compliance. The bulk of the personnel actions in the federal government were taken by the dozens of departments and agencies that make up the executive branch, operating within the laws, rules and regulations, and under the watchful eye of the Civil Service Commission as well as with its advice, assistance, and stimulation. It was the administrators who actually appointed, assigned, promoted, transferred, trained, disciplined, and discharged government employees. After 1938, by presidential order, each major agency had a personnel office, headed by an agency personnel officer, to assist in these functions at the agency level and to serve as liaison with the Commission. In practice, however, the Commission played a key role initiating most of the legislation and Executive Orders under which it operates, its views were invariably solicited when any other source initiated proposals, it was consulted by the heads of other agencies who did not want to run afoul of its enforcement powers, and it enjoyed strong support among civic organizations and among unions and associations of federal workers. From 1958 on, its members have had six year, overlapping terms instead of serving at the pleasure of the President. In the partitioned world of federal personnel management, there was probably no single dominant force, but the Civil Service Commission was unquestionably the central figure.

The government organization in charge of logistics is the General Services Administration. A list of the major units of GSA gives some idea of the range of its responsibilities:

Federal Supply Service
Defense Materials Service (stockpiles)
Public Building Service
Transportation and Communication Service
Utilization and Disposal Service
National Archives and Records Service

The list, however, does not make clear the control responsibilities of the GSA; they are important. Executive branch agencies may not acquire whatever supplies they wish; they must take supplies of the quality provided by the Supply Service and in the quantities allocated by GSA. Agencies are not free to acquire their own space but must occupy space occupied and managed by the Public Buildings Service. Federal agencies must rely on automobiles and communications facilities provided by the Transportation and Communication Service, and what they do with their records is of interest to the National Archives and Records Service. The power of the GSA should not of course be overstated; within its area of responsibility there is room for negotiation and bargaining and indeed evasion. GSA no more has absolute control over agencies than does the Bureau of the Budget or the Civil Service Commission. But when the Bureau of the Budget and the President are on its side, its rules and regulations cannot be ignored with impunity.

Conclusion

Perusal of the structure of the Executive Branch may leave one with an Alice-in-Wonderland feeling. Quite different names may be applied to essentially similar organizations, and the same labels may adorn quite different organizations. Tradition and fashion, status and prestige have much to do with the names of organizations. Names may linger when substance changes and may change when substance goes unchanged. (The Agency for International Development has gone through several names since World War II; familiar wine keeps getting poured into different bottles.) If all this sounds confusing, it is. But one point is clear: merely knowing the formal designation of an organization—whether department, administration, bureau, or office—tells little about size, structure, resources, or mission. The Federal Security Agency was a welfare agency; the National Security Agency is an intelligence agency in the Department of Defense.

Notes for Chapter 2

1. A number of articles deal with the Bureau of the Budget. See Arthur A. Maass, "In Accord with the Program of the President?" *Public Policy* (1953), pp. 77–93; Fritz Morstein Marx, "The Bureau of the Budget: Its Evolution and Present Role," *American Political Science Review*, vol. 39 (August and October 1945), pp. 653–684, 869–898; Richard E. Neustadt, "Presidency and Legislation: The Growth of Central Clearance," *American Political Science Review*, vol. 48 (September 1954), pp. 641–671 and "Presidency and Legislation: Planning the

President's Program," *American Political Science Review,* vol. 49 (December 1955), pp. 980–1021; James W. Davis and Randall B. Ripley, "The Bureau of the Budget and Executive Branch Agencies: Notes on Their Interaction," *Journal of Politics,* vol. 29 (November 1967), pp. 749–769.

2. For an account of the Council of Economic Advisers see Edward S. Flash, Jr., *Economic Advice and Presidential Leadership* (New York: Columbia University Press, 1965).

3. In *Economic Report of the President,* January 1966 (Washington: U.S. Government Printing Office, 1966), p. 195.

4. Title I, Section 101 of the National Security Act of 1947 as amended. Reprinted in Senator Henry M. Jackson, *The National Security Council:* Jackson Sub-Committee Papers on Policy Making at the Presidential Level (New York: Praeger, 1965), p. 296.

5. In Jackson, *The National Security Council.* See testimony of Robert Cutler, p. 112; letters from Bundy to Jackson, p. 276 and p. 279.

6. Hearings before the Select Committee on Government Research of the House of Representatives, 88th Congress, 1st session, p. 261. For more about the Office of Science and Technology see Jerome B. Wiesner, *Where Science and Politics Meet* (New York: McGraw Hill, 1965.) For a recent brief discussion see "The Hornig Years: Did LBJ Neglect His Science Advisor?" *Science,* 31 January 1969, pp. 453–458.

7. The literature on regulatory agencies is vast. Marver Bernstein, *Regulating Business by Independent Commission* (Princeton: Princeton University Press, 1955) is a good introduction to the subject. A brief survey is provided by James Fesler, "Independent Regulatory Agencies," in Fritz Morstein Marx, *Elements of Public Administration* (Englewood Cliffs, N.J.: Prentice-Hall, Inc., 1959), pp. 191–218.

8. For an introduction to government corporations see V. O. Key, Jr., "Government Corporations," in Marx, *Elements of Public Administration,* pp. 219–245. See also Harold Seidman, "The Theory of the Autonomous Government Corporation: A Critical Appraisal," *Public Administration Review,* XII (1952), pp. 89–96, and also his "The Government Corporation: Organization and Control," *Public Administration Review* XIV (1954), pp. 183–192.

9. V. O. Key, *op. cit.,* p. 220.

10. *Ibid.*, p. 224.

11. O. Glenn Stahl, *Public Personnel Administration* (New York: Harper & Row, 1962, 5th ed.) pp. 425–426.

12. Herbert Kaufman, "The Growth of the Federal Personnel System," in Wallace Sayre (ed.), *The Federal Government Service* (Englewood Cliffs, N.J.: Prentice-Hall, Inc., 1965), p. 56. By permission of the publisher.

★★★
PERSONNEL IN THE EXECUTIVE BRANCH

THE EXECUTIVE BRANCH consists of millions of people performing a variety of tasks. This chapter focuses on these people, the employees of Executive Branch organizations. It begins with illustrative data on the numbers and types of federal employees and goes on to consider such topics as recruitment, the political activity of public employees, and public employee unions.

The Work Force

The federal government is the largest single employer in the nation. As Table 3–1 makes clear, there

Notes for this chapter appear on pages 76–78.

are almost 3,000,000 civilian government employees; and almost all of them work in the Executive Branch.

TABLE 3–1   Employees in Legislative, Judicial, and Executive Branches

Branch	1955	1960	1965	1968
Legislative	21,711	22,886	25,947	27,870
Judicial	4,136	4,992	5,904	6,486
Executive	2,371,462	2,370,826	2,496,090	2,906,588
Totals	2,397,309	2,398,704	2,527,941	2,940,944

SOURCE: *Statistical Abstract of the United States, 1969, Table No. 569, page 398.*

Table 3–2 provides a detailed breakdown of Executive Branch employment; it emphasizes the variety and complexity of the Executive Branch. The Department of Defense and the Post Office employ hundreds of thousands; many executive boards and commissions employ only hundreds.

TABLE 3–2   Civilian Employment in Executive Branch Agencies, 1968

Agency	Number of Employees
Executive Office of the President	
White House Office	274
Bureau of the Budget	547
Executive Mansion and Grounds	70
National Security Council	38
Office of Economic Opportunity	2,938
Office of Emergency Planning	417
Office of Science and Technology	71
All other	327
Executive Departments	
Agriculture	108,318
Commerce	35,453

Defense
  Office of the Secretary   2,621
  Department of the Army   465,879
  Department of the Navy   412,559
  Department of the Air Force   316,419
  Other defense activities   69,674
Health, Education and Welfare   107,805
Housing and Urban Development   14,559
Interior   69,417
Justice   33,653
Labor   9,882
Post Office   715,970
State   47,429
  Agency for International Development   18,017
  Peace Corps   1,713
Transportation   57,929
Treasury   92,431

Independent Agencies

American Battle Monuments Commission   440
Arms Control and Disarmament Agency   181
Atomic Energy Commission   7,267
Board of Governors, Federal Reserve System   754
Canal Zone Government   3,286
Civil Aeronautics Board   643
Civil Service Commission   5,396
Commission on Civil Rights   169
Equal Employment Opportunity Commission   398
Export-Import Bank   301
Farm Credit Administration   232
Federal Communications Commission   .1,504
Federal Deposit Insurance Corporation   1,859
Federal Home Loan Bank Board   1,274
Federal Maritime Commission   250
Federal Mediation and Conciliation Service   436
Federal Power Commission   1,093
Federal Trade Commission   1,194
Federal Claims Settlement Commission   107
General Services Administration   38,673
Information Agency   11,797
Interstate Commerce Commission   1,864
National Aeronautics and Space Administration   33,589
National Capital Housing Authority   792
National Labor Relations Board   2,367
National Mediation Board   131

National Science Foundation	1,075
Panama Canal Company	13,059
Railroad Retirement Board	1,709
Renegotiation Board	171
Securities and Exchange Commission	1,376
Selective Service System	8,940
Small Business Administration	4,413
Smithsonian Institution	2,416
Soldiers' Home	1,096
Tariff Commission	271
Tax Court of the United States	161
Tennessee Valley Authority	18,535
Veterans' Administration	172,217
All other	472

SOURCE: *Statistical Abstract of the United States, 1969, Table No. 569,* p. *398.*

Employees of the Executive Branch are distributed not only among many organizations but also throughout the United States. A glance at the telephone book of any city will reveal many federal organizations. The State of California contains more federal employees than the Washington, D.C., metropolitan area; and Illinois, New York, Texas, and Pennsylvania all have well over 100,000 federal employees within their borders. Table 3–3 shows the distribution of federal employment on a

TABLE 3–3   Paid Civilian Employment of the Federal Government by State— 1967

State	Number of Federal Employees
Alabama	56,865
Alaska	14,344
Arizona	25,852
Arkansas	16,266
California	317,867
Colorado	41,645
Connecticut	18,557
Delaware	4,283

Florida	68,351
Georgia	76,812
Hawaii	27,515
Idaho	7,613
Illinois	113,699
Indiana	41,633
Iowa	17,602
Kansas	21,606
Kentucky	37,834
Louisiana	28,679
Maine	16,834
Maryland	62,179
Massachusetts	66,472
Michigan	53,524
Minnesota	28,984
Mississippi	19,742
Missouri	65,148
Montana	10,431
Nebraska	14,844
Nevada	8,011
New Hampshire	4,721
New Jersey	67,436
New Mexico	25,789
New York	182,392
North Carolina	36,536
North Dakota	7,318
Ohio	98,344
Oklahoma	55,108
Oregon	23,904
Pennsylvania	143,108
Rhode Island	14,948
South Carolina	30,080
South Dakota	9,239
Tennessee	40,076
Texas	147,248
Utah	41,627
Vermont	3,329
Virginia	79,746
Washington	56,839
West Virginia	12,496
Wisconsin	24,296
Wyoming	4,829
Washington, D.C., metropolitan area	311,986
Outside the United States	243,148

SOURCE: *Statistical Abstract of the United States, 1969, Table No. 571, page 400.*

state-by-state basis. One implication of these data is that federal government is not necessarily government by some bureaucrat in far-off Washington, D.C. Indeed, federal employees located throughout the United States and working where they live may be just as aware of local conditions as comparable state and local government employees.

Federal employees hold a variety of jobs. The Executive Branch is not composed largely of clerks. Today scientists, engineers, economists, lawyers, doctors, and educators all work for the federal government. A recent analysis by the Bureau of the Budget reported:

> Changes have taken place in the position structure as a result of changes in the character of the Government's workload and in the employee skills required to deal with it. For example, between 1954 and 1965, greater specialization and emphasis on research and development led to an increase of 53 per cent in the number of engineers in the Federal Service, and an 83 per cent increase in the number of physical scientists. During this period, the Government's need for professional medical personnel rose 31 per cent and for biological scientists, 46 per cent. At the same time, the expanded efforts to reduce employment and to increase productivity—in many cases by shifting from manual to semi-automatic or automatic processing methods—decreased the need for unskilled employees.
>
> A recent analysis by the Civil Service Commission shows the following changes in position structure of Classification Act employees between 1961 and 1965:
>
> Reduction in percentage of clerical and aide jobs . . . from 53.2 per cent to 47.3 per cent of total employment. Increase in percentage of professional, technical, and administrative jobs . . . from 46.7 to 52.4 per cent of total employment.[1]

A somewhat fuller picture of the variety of occupations in the Executive Branch is provided by Table 3–4. Postal occupations account for by far the largest number of white-collar jobs, but there are substantial numbers of employees in other occupational groups. (There are also a number of employees in a variety of blue collar occupations, but data showing the distribution of the blue collar work force is not included here.)

TABLE 3–4 White Collar Federal Employees by Major Occupational Group—1967

Occupation	Number of Employees
Postal	568,250
General administration, clerical and office services	456,327
Engineering and architecture	144,592
Accounting and budget	112,965
Medical, hospital, dental, and public health	96,164
Supply	82,086
Business and industry	53,663
Legal and kindred	44,697
Physical sciences	42,577
Biological sciences	41,926
Personnel management and industrial relations	37,089
Investigation	34,592
Social science, psychology, and welfare	33,204
Transportation	32,689
Education	24,269
Commodity quality control, inspection and grading	21,062
Information and arts	20,060
Equipment, facilities, and service	19,197
Mathematics and statistics	15,636
Library and archives	7,717
Veterinary medical service	2,393
Copyright, patent, and trade-mark	1,790
Miscellaneous occupations	39,565

SOURCE: *Statistical Abstract of the United States, 1969, Table 574,* p. 402.

Looking at statistics such as those in Table 3–4 helps to answer the question, "What do federal employees do?" To cast more light on this question, John J. Corson and R. Shale Paul inquired specifically (by means of questionnaires and interviews) into the activities of the top 5,000 career civil servants.[2] They were able to classify these senior civil servants into three main groups. Thirty-five per cent of the top civil servants were classified as program managers; that is, they served as bureau chiefs or division directors or office heads and were responsible for carrying out programs. Another 35 per cent were engaged in such activities as budgeting, personnel administration, management analysis, or other types of administrative support work. The remaining 30 per cent were working simply as professionals—lawyers, economists, scientists, engineers, and so on.

The Personnel Systems of the Executive Branch

In the preceding section the Executive Branch was viewed as one large employer, with employees scattered among different organizations. In practice, the Executive Branch becomes several distinct employers or, more accurately, several distinct personnel systems.

The rules of the United States Civil Service Commission govern the entrance requirements and conditions of work for more than two million government employees in the competitive civil service. About half of these employees are covered by the Classification Act, and their salaries are determined by legislation. About a quarter of the employees are blue-collar workers, and their salaries are determined by local wage boards.

They are paid at rates comparable to those prevailing in the communities where they work. The remaining several hundred thousand employees are postal workers, and the Postal Field Service salary system determines the rates at which these employees are paid.

Most organizations in the Executive Branch use employees who are in the competitive civil service, but some organizations have their own merit systems and are not controlled by the Civil Service Commission. They have their own rules and standards for hiring, retaining, promoting, and dismissing. (It should be pointed out, however, that in the last several years, beginning with the Salary Act of 1962, an attempt has been made to ensure that employees in different systems who do equivalent work are paid equivalent rates.) The FBI, for example, has its own merit system, as do the Central Intelligence Agency and the National Security Agency. The Atomic Energy Commission has its own personnel system, and so does the Tennessee Valley Authority. The Foreign Service in the Department of State is separate from the regular civil service. The uniformed services are of course not part of the civil service; besides the regular armed forces, they include the Coast Guard, the Coast and Geodetic Survey, and the Public Health Service. The Department of Medicine and Surgery in the Veterans' Administration is also separate from the regular civil service.

Why do these separate systems exist? A common argument, and one that is often justified, is that some organizations have unique needs and problems and the general rules of the Civil Service Commission may be too restrictive. The argument is that if an organization is bound by Civil Service Commission rules it cannot hire people it needs and cannot as freely dismiss unsatisfactory employees.

Recruitment of Career Employees

Since 1883 increasing numbers of civil servants have been recruited by means of competitive examinations.[3] When the Pendleton Act was first passed not more than 15 per cent of the federal work force was included under its provisions, but now more than 85 per cent is. Today the government announces more than 20,000 examinations, processes almost 2,000,000 applications, and hires well over 200,000 people a year. Most of the examinations are given by the various agencies of the Executive Branch under the supervision of the Civil Service Commission. "Of the 300,000 appointments to the competitive service in 1962, more than 85 per cent were recruited and examined by boards of examiners within the departments and agencies themselves."[4]

Quoting a few examination announcements may help to illustrate both the variety of personnel recruited and the decentralized nature of the recruitment process.[5]

United States Civil Service Commission announces examination for geologist, grades and salaries GS-9, $7,479 [through] GS-15, $17,055, apply to Executive Secretary, Board of U.S. Civil Service Examiners, Geological Survey, Department of the Interior, Washington, D.C.

United States Civil Service Commission announces examination for radio announcers for international broadcasting in English, salaries GS-9, $7,479 [through] GS-12, $10,019, apply to Executive Secretary, Board of Civil Service Examiners, U.S. Information Agency, Washington, D.C.

United States Civil Service Commission announces examination for medical technologist $5,181 to $8,961 a year (grades GS-5 through GS-11), for duty in Veterans Administration installations.

United States Civil Service Commission announces examination for operations research analyst, $7,987– 17,055 a year (grades 9–15), announcement 193 B . . . . Apply to Executive Secretary, Board of Civil Service Examiners, Bolling Air Force Base, Washington, D.C.

Most federal civilian personnel are examined through the departments and agencies, but not all are. Some examinations designed to select administrative and professional employees are administered directly by the Civil Service Commission. Among the most interesting of these and probably one of the better known (at least among college students) is the Federal Service Entrance Examination (the FSEE), an examination designed for college graduates who are interested in a career in a federal agency. It was first offered in 1955 replacing more than 100 examinations previously given by the federal government. Liberal arts graduates seeking federal employment now take this one examination. It is administered several times a year at numerous locations throughout the United States and applications are taken continuously. An applicant may also take a Management Interne examination. If an applicant passes both these examinations he can be considered for a higher grade and is frequently offered the opportunity of participating in a management training program.

Examinations, of course, are only one part of the whole recruitment process. The process, in briefest outline, has been described as follows:[6]

> On the basis of requests for eligibles from agencies, examinations are planned and scheduled.
>
> Examinations are publicly announced.
>
> Candidates must submit applications.
>
> Applications are reviewed and candidates are notified of their eligibility.
>
> Examinations are given.

Examinations are graded and eligible registers are set up for those that pass in rank order of grade.

In response to an agency request, the top three names on the register are certified.

The agency selects and appoints one of the three.

Although this outline may make the recruitment of federal employees seem a fairly straightforward process, a number of problems or questions remain. One continuing problem is whether the tests actually select people who can do the job best. This problem really has three parts: (1) What is the nature of the job in question? (2) What skills, aptitudes, knowledge, and attitudes are required to do it? (3) Does the recruiting test being used actually measure these?

These questions may be fairly simple to answer if clerical jobs are in question. Obviously a typist may need to type 60 words per minute, and performance tests measuring this ability are simple to design. Other clerical and some blue-collar positions may be equally amenable to examination. But what about a management analyst, a budget examiner, an investigator, a physicist, or an air traffic controller? What aptitudes and attitudes and knowledge are required by these jobs, and how can they be measured, or even detected? The Civil Service Commission does continuing research on such problems, but it is aware that not enough is known. It recognizes that the more complex the job to be filled (and this includes most administrative and professional positions) the more difficult informed recruiting is.

In a listing a few years ago of personnel research problems the Commission defined two other recruiting problems.[7]

While present methods are relatively successful, they are aimed at selecting persons with the required skills and abilities to perform traditional duties in a traditional manner. However, there is a need to identify employees who would be capable of finding new ways to perform work or who would be motivated to perform in an outstanding manner. New methods are needed to select supervisors who have the ability to motivate employees and to encourage creativity.

• • •

The process of applying for a government job is weighted heavily in favor of the candidate who doesn't mind filling out numerous and voluminous application forms; who doesn't mind listing every job he's ever had, and every place he has ever lived, and who doesn't mind signing an affidavit witnessed by a notary public attesting that he is really a resident of some state that isn't over its apportionment quota; etc.

Perhaps there are a number of creative types, so badly needed in Government, who are repelled by the nature of the hiring process; who see in it a confirmation of their worst fears of "Government bureaucracy." New techniques need to be developed to reach these people.

This problem of application procedures is one about which very little is known. We do not even know how significant it is, but it seems important to find out. Examinations, even when they are valid and reliable, can identify only the most competent of those people who choose to take them. Some very able potential employees may not bother to take the examination. Why?

Another problem relating to the examination process should be mentioned. For which jobs are competitive examinations appropriate? And for which should there be either no competition or no examination of any kind? Some generalizations in this area are worth noting. Positions with highly technical duties for which there are few qualified applicants may not be filled through competitive examination. However, an "unassembled examination" may be used. That is, the experience and qualifications of the job applicant may be evaluated to see if they enable him to fill the position in question. For other positions even this form of examination may not be used. Confidential or policy-making positions may be exempt from all examinations, as may part-time or temporary positions. The real problem is not whether in principle some positions may be exempted from examinations, but rather how many and which positions are to be exempted. Here there is room for substantial conflict.

Two other recruitment problems have more to do with the nature of the federal service than with the examination process. In 1964 Franklin Kilpatrick, Milton Cummings, and Kent Jennings in their book, *The Image of the Federal Service,* dealt with one serious problem—the unattractiveness of federal employment to many able people.

> The appeal of federal employment is lowest among those kinds of employed adults for whom the government's qualitative needs are the greatest and for whom the competition will be keenest in the future. In general, those persons with better education, higher occupational attainments, and more technical skills feel that federal employment would seriously lower their occupational satisfaction. On the other hand, those with less education, lower occupational attainments, and less technical skills feel that government would not seriously hurt their occupational satisfaction, and would, in some cases, raise it.[8]

College students and graduate students also tended to feel that federal employment would be less advantageous for them than other positions they expected to take.

Related to these findings, the authors point out that job security, steady income, and retirement benefits are what people think the federal employment has to offer, but these benefits are congruent with the values of people with lower, not higher, levels of attainment.[9] In other words, federal employment seems to appeal most to those the government has the least difficulty finding. It appeals least to those who are the scarcest and hardest to recruit. Now certainly there are many exceptions to these findings. The federal government, particularly some agencies such as the Bureau of the Budget, the Department of Defense, the Department of Housing and Urban Development, and the Central Intelligence Agency, does succeed in attracting and keeping able people. But the *Image of the Federal Service* points out an important recruitment problem.

Another problem affects retention even more than recruitment, and that is pay. In recent years an effort has been made to make federal pay comparable to wages paid to employees doing similar work outside the federal government. The 1962 Pay Bill and subsequent bills took important steps in that direction, and as a consequence employees in the lower and middle ranges of the federal service are paid about what their counterparts outside the government are paid. In the higher levels of the civil service, however, comparability still does not exist. The result is that some qualified people choose not to work for the government because they see a lack of salary potential, and others may leave the federal service because they can make more money elsewhere.

This latter proposition is supported both by the findings in the *Image of the Federal Service* and by David T. Stanley's book, *The Higher Civil Service*. Kilpatrick and his associates report that in samples of federal executives, natural and social scientists, and engineers, 58 per cent to 75 per cent report that financial rewards would be better outside the government.[10]

Stanley's book contains the data in Table 3–5; they suggest clearly the financial gap that exists between high-level government employment and private employment.

TABLE 3–5   Why Respondents Think Others
Leave Higher Civil Service

Reasons	Present Employees (N 263)	Former Employees (N 80)
More money	70%	56%
New opportunities	27	30
Frustrations: red tape, budget, slow decisions	14	43
Few leave except to retire	25	10
Political reasons	5	24

SOURCE: *Adapted from Table 5.4 in David T. Stanley,* The Higher Civil Service *(Washington: The Brookings Institution, 1964), p. 67.*

Until the pay problem and the image problem are both solved, the federal government may have difficulty recruiting the administrative, professional, and technical staff that it needs. And since the government needs more and more of these people, its recruiting problems may grow more acute.

Recruitment of Political Appointees

Many of the most important positions in the Executive Branch at Cabinet and sub-Cabinet level are filled by the President directly. Article II, Section 2 of the United States Constitution, which deals with the President's appointment power, says:

He shall nominate and by and with the advice and consent of the Senate, shall appoint ambassadors, other public ministers and consuls, judges of the Supreme Court, and all other officers of the United States whose appointments are not herein otherwise provided for, and which shall be established by law; but the Congress may by law vest the appointment of such inferior officers, as they think proper, in the President alone, in the courts of law, or in the heads of departments.

The President shall have power to fill up all vacancies that may happen during the recess of the Senate, by granting commissions which shall expire at the end of their next session.

Pursuant to these provisions the President appoints Cabinet Secretaries and sub-Cabinet officials, heads of independent agencies and regulatory commissions, some bureau chiefs, and scores of other officials. With a few exceptions the President's power to appoint is qualified by the Senate's power to consent or demur, but this qualification is often not a crucial one, particularly for major posts. The President has the initiative and the Senate demurs infrequently. Partially, of course, this is because the President is unlikely to nominate someone he thinks the Senate is unlikely to approve.

Although the President has the power to appoint, he in effect must share this power. Interest groups, the President's party, state Congressional delegations, the President's own advisors, and members of the Cabinet, to say nothing of the press, may all have views that they do not shy from expressing. The President cannot heed everyone, but he is unlikely to ignore everyone. Perhaps it is a rule that the closer an appointee will be to the President the more a President's own wishes may control, and the more distant the appointee (a state director of Selective Service, a United States Marshall, the Ambassador to Upper Volta) the less relevant may be the President's desires and indeed the less may be his interest. It should be understood that when the President does not appoint a man of his own choice, a man who shares his views, he may make more difficult for himself the task of influencing the direction of policy and program. But it should also be understood that when a President makes appointments he may be trying to gain Congressional votes and group and public support. These he may need as much as he needs efficiency, economy, and competence.

Two studies that shed some light on the political appointment process are Richard Fenno's *The President's Cabinet*[11] and Dean Mann's *The Assistant Secretaries*.[12] Fenno's wide-ranging book includes a chapter on Cabinet appointments that is quite informative.[13] Discussing in some detail the variables that affect appointment, Fenno illustrates clearly how complex, varied, and hard to describe the political appointment process is. In his discussion he gives attention to availability and balance. He asks and answers the question, "Who is available for Cabinet office?" He suggests that availability is made up of five factors: party, personal loyalty, geography, socio-economic factors, and specialized talents.

Although membership in the President's party is usually thought of as a *sine qua non,* it is not always a requirement and it is certainly not sufficient. American parties are too varied for party identification to mean a great deal in terms of policy preference. Robert McNamara and Douglas Dillon, both Republicans, appeared comfortable in the Cabinet of President John F. Kennedy, a Democrat, and clearly McGeorge Bundy, another Republican, was happy as a Kennedy aide in the White House Office. But it must be admitted that it is conventional for a President to give Cabinet posts— particularly those dealing with domestic matters—to members of his own party. Some posts almost always go to party members. The position of Postmaster General is commonly held by a prominent party leader or national chairman. The position of Attorney General is also often a political post. In other positions other qualifications may outweigh in importance party identification; and national security and diplomatic posts are more likely than any others to go to members of the opposition.

Personal loyalty is another qualification, but given the fact that many Presidents have appointed virtual strangers to Cabinet posts it cannot be rated as terribly important. It is surely more important for retention in a Cabinet post than for initial appointment. For some posts geographic residence may be important. The Secretary of the Interior often comes from the West and the Secretary of Agriculture from an agricultural area. Iowa has produced more Secretaries of Agriculture than any other state. The Secretaries of Commerce and Labor ordinarily come from industrial states. Of course it is not enough that a prospective Cabinet member come from the appropriate area; he must also be supported by the appropriate groups—whether business, labor, or agriculture.

What can be said about the importance of specialized talent? Although this may be more important at the sub-Cabinet level (it is, for example, inconceivable that the Assistant Secretary for Science and Technology in the Department of Commerce would not be a scientist), specialized talent cannot be neglected at the Cabinet level. The most obvious case is the Attorney General's position—the occupant must be a lawyer. The Secretary of State often, though by no means always, has wide experience in international affairs and diplomacy. Increasingly, management sophistication seems not only relevant but necessary in the Department of

Defense. Financial experience is often sought when a Secretary of the Treasury is recruited. Surely in some cases appropriate skills and experience are more definable than in others, but most posts are likely to be associated with some particular mix of skills and experience. Still, any President is fairly free to do what he chooses in the matter. He may, for instance, appoint as a secretary a man with political experience and then select a deputy who can provide management strength.

With all these factors to consider—does a prospective Cabinet member belong to the party, will he be loyal, does he come from the right section of the country and is he supported by the necessary groups, does he have appropriate competence—a President must consider one more: How will the appointee fit into the Cabinet? Will there be too many businessmen? Too many easterners? No Catholics at all? There is of course no particular figure which the President may not exceed, and no figure he must reach. But he does have to be sensitive to the appearance of the Cabinet. Does it present a balanced appearance or for one reason or another does it seem lopsided or unrepresentative? A President cannot be concerned only with the individual characteristics of a potential Cabinet member; he must also consider how each one will fit into the whole.

Dean Mann has explored in detail the appointment of sub-Cabinet officials in his book, *The Assistant Secretaries*. His research, assisted by Jameson W. Doig, makes clear that presidential appointments are likely to be presidential in form only.

> Although the recruitment process in each administration reflects the personality and political orientation of its Chief Executive, practice and expediency dictate that presidential control over appointments has to be shared with others who also have a stake in the administrative branch of the government. In some instances,

even for appointments only two echelons below the President, his responsibility has been delegated to such a degree that he has often been able only to ratify (and with rarity, to veto) choices made by others.[14]

Who are these others? The most important "others" are agency and department heads who may and often do select their own subordinates. That they do not always do so was illustrated by the appointment of Adlai Stevenson as Ambassador to the United Nations before Dean Rusk, his nominal superior, was appointed Secretary of State. But such is not the rule. Ordinarily department heads have a voice in choosing their subordinates. Party officials may also play a part in selecting or approving sub-Cabinet officials and so, too, may pressure-group leaders. Congressmen have their favorites. Although the part played by Congressmen and by party and pressure group representatives is usually not so great as the part played by the President and by department and agency heads, their interest does mean that sub-Cabinet appointments, just like Cabinet posts, may be the subject of some negotiation. Trades may be made, and some bargains struck.

This is not to say that every job is hotly contested, but merely that Presidents and Cabinet Secretaries cannot do precisely as they please. Rather, they operate within looser or tighter limits. A well-organized and influential clientele may tighten the limits; a relatively invisible post may be filled largely at the pleasure of the recruiter. A President may give some jobs to personal friends and long-time supporters. A Secretary may do likewise. But the demands of politics and policy militate against all or indeed many posts being filled in this friendly way. Some posts will inevitably be filled by total strangers and others by political antagonists.

It is hard to go beyond these few general points.

As Mann and Doig emphasize, the recruitment process is diverse and complex—and given the numbers of posts involved, the numbers of policy and program areas, and the variety of Presidents it could be no other way. An additional observation from *The Assistant Secretaries* is in order here.

> The selection of men for the second echelon of the President's executive team reflects many of the basic characteristics and values of the American political system. Having responded over the years to the cross pressures of conflicting interests—executive and legislative, business and professional, public and private—the process appears haphazard, for no formal procedure has been devised for locating, classifying, and enticing qualified men into these positions. An even more important point is that no system has been evolved for preparing potential candidates adequately for their duties in office. As a result, the government is largely dependent on untrained people to fill its policy-making positions.[15]

This situation may have adverse consequences for the quality of governmental decision-making. It may also mean that career people, who are trained and experienced, may be called on for advice and decisions more often than they otherwise would be. The inexperience and brief tenure of political appointees mean that much important work is in the hands of career civil servants.

Presidential Dismissals

To the President's power to appoint is coupled the power to dismiss, but this also is qualified. Not all the President's appointees serve until his displeasure or, as it is more commonly put, at his pleasure. If all their terms were in fact so limited the tenure of some officials would probably have been less than it has been. The term of the Chairman of the Federal Reserve Board is fixed by law. So are the terms of commissioners on such bodies as the Interstate Commerce Commission, the Federal Communications Commission, and the Federal Power Commission. In a sense the President can only hire these men, not fire them. Many other appointees serve by law at the pleasure of the President, but in practice their tenure is not so limited. To be sure the President's legal right to fire executive officers and without the advice or consent of the Senate is fairly clear and has been so since at least 1926, when the Supreme Court decided *Myers v. United States.* The phrase "fairly clear" is used purposely; in another and later case, *Humphrey's Executor v. United States* (1935), the court held that a member of the Federal Trade Commission could not be dismissed; and other cases have also qualified the President's power to dismiss.

But the legal obstacles to dismissing subordinates are probably less impressive than the political obstacles. The President, for practical purposes, is no more free to fire at will than he is to hire at will. President Truman was on solid legal footing when he dismissed General MacArthur; yet he met a storm of opposition. Any President could dismiss J. Edgar Hoover; no President has and not only because of Mr. Hoover's presumed competence. In 1966 the furor over the apparent dismissal of Abba Schwartz from his post as administrator in the State Department's Bureau of Security and Consular Affairs reminded the President that prominent officials cannot be let go unnoticed.[16] Dismissals, quite as much as appointments, are of interest to many participants in the political arena.

Political Activity of Public Employees

Although career employees in the Executive Branch may engage in some of the partisan political activities open to other citizens, there are certain restrictions on such activities. Career employees may vote and express their opinions privately on political matters, but they may not engage in overt partisan activity or act as the public representative of a party or faction.

> No person employed in the executive branch of the federal government, or any agency or department thereof, shall use his official authority or influence for the purpose of interfering with an election or effecting the result thereof. No person occupying a position in the competitive service shall take any active part in political management or political campaigns, except as may be provided by or pursuant to statute. All such persons shall retain the right to vote as they may choose and to express their opinions on all political subjects and candidates.[17]

A number of other activities are specifically prohibited. The Hatch Act of 1939, which forbade political activity for civil servants, gave the force of law to a long array of Civil Service Commission decisions and rules permitting or prohibiting a variety of specific activities. For example, career employees may not solicit contributions for campaigns or be compelled to contribute to campaigns. They may not be delegates to party conventions or serve on party committees or run for public office.

Why do the rules governing partisan political activity exist? The rules exist partially as a reaction to the spoils system and represent an attempt to neutralize the civil service. Moreover, it could be argued that they represent a Congressional attempt to weaken the power of the President and to protect Congressmen. Imagine how powerful the President might be if he could turn two and a half million civil servants into workers for his party and financial contributors to it. Imagine the position of Congressmen if civil servants could be organized to vote them out of office. Imagine these events, and it is easy to understand the legislation and regulations that limit the political activity of career civil servants. Another reason or justification for the limitations is that career employees, particularly upper-level career employees, have to work closely with political appointees who are members of one party or another. Communication and cooperation between political appointees and career civil servants may be easier when the career men are not publicly identified with and committed to a particular party. Republicans may have enough difficulty working with career officials who have just worked with and for Democratic office holders for eight years. If the career officials had publicly supported the Democrats and campaigned for them, the difficulties would be greater; cooperation might be completely impossible.

One may also ask how effective the rules are, but to this question there are no clear answers, and no research on the extensiveness of violations appears to have been done. If we assume that to be effective regulations must be understood, then it would appear that many of the regulations are not very effective. As Table 3–6 shows, data collected for the Commission on Political Activity of Government Personnel show clearly that there there is much confusion about what is permitted and what is not. As the Commission said in its report, "64.1 per cent of the Federal employees understand five or less of the restrictions in the law. Only 35.8 per cent

TABLE 3–6   Percentage Responses of Federal
Employees As to What Political
Activities They Think They
"Can" and "Cannot" Do Under
Present Hatch Act Rules

Activity	Can	Cannot	Not Sure
a. Make a speech at a rally held by a political party	15.8	69.4	14.6
b. Put a political sticker on his own car	63.0	24.4	12.5
c. Hold office in a political party organization	8.5	80.6	10.7
d. Run for state or national office	8.9	81.0	9.6
e. Write a letter to his senator or congressman	96.0	1.5	2.2
f. Drive people to the polls on election day	45.0	40.5	14.2
g. Run for a school board position where people are not candidates of either major political party	66.5	15.8	17.3
h. Become actively involved in local issues such as civil rights and taxes	49.5	32.6	17.3
i. Participate in voter registration drives	48.1	35.6	16.0
j. Distribute campaign materials for a party or candidate	18.6	71.2	10.1

SOURCE: *Report of the Commission on Political Activity of Government Personnel, Findings and Recommendations, Volume One, Table 1. The data were collected and analyzed for the Commission by the Survey Research Center of the University of Michigan. Items a, c, d, f, i, and j are prohibited by law and the rest are permitted.*

understand six or more of the restrictions and no employee understands more than eight out of the ten."[18] In other words no employee surveyed responded correctly to all ten items. Because of this confusion the Commission recommended a simplification and liberalization of the present Civil Service Commission rules governing political activity.

Faced with compelling evidence that the existing law unduly confuses and restricts more than 4.5 million Federal, State, and local public employees, this Commission proposes a new approach. It recommends that Congress eliminate the confusing array of do's and don'ts by clearly defining permitted activities and prohibitions in the statute. The prohibitions would be only those that Congress finds necessary to protect employees against actions that would threaten the integrity, efficiency, and impartiality of the public service.[19]

There might well be some risk in such a policy, but it should be remembered that at least some civil servants engage in prohibited activities now, if only because they do not know they are prohibited, and government does not seem much the worse for it. Most citizens of the United States, even though under no restrictions, do little more than vote. Unless it is assumed that civil servants as a group are substantially different from most citizens, it is safe to assume that even if the law is liberalized most civil servants will continue to do little more than vote.

It should be made clear in closing this section that political appointees are not subject to the restrictions that limit the political activity of career civil servants. Indeed they are often *expected* to be politically active and of course often hold their positions just because they have been politically active. They are commonly expected to contribute to the party war chest and to attend dinners and rallies. They may speak in support of the policies of the administration and in support of their party, and they may defend themselves and the administration before Congress. Precisely how active political appointees are depends on their own predilections, the position they hold, and the views of the President they serve. What is certain is that no political appointee could attack in public the policies of the party in power and continue to hold his position. If political activity, in other words, appeared to conflict with loyalty to the administration, it would be curtailed or the appointee would be dismissed.

Public Employee Unions

Not all federal employees are members of unions, but many are; and their organized activities have an impact on the personnel policies and practices followed in the Executive Branch. Craft and trade unions are represented in the Executive Branch by unions of printers, machinists, carpenters. There are several postal unions, other unions limited to specific government organizations, and government-wide unions. This list illustrates the number and variety of government unions:

POSTAL UNIONS
    National Association of Special Delivery
        Messengers
    National Federation of Post Office Motor
        Vehicle Employees
    National Postal Union
    United Federation of Postal Clerks
    National Rural Letter Carrier's Association
    National Association of Letter Carriers
    National Association of Post Office and Postal
        Transportation Service Handlers, Watchmen,
        Messengers, and Group Leaders
    National Association of Post Office and General
        Services Maintenance Employees
    United Federation of Postal Clerks
    National Association of Postal Supervisors
    National Association of Postmasters
    National League of Postmasters

SPECIFIC UNIONS
  National Association of Internal Revenue
    Employees
  National Association of ASCE County Office
    Employees
  Patent Office Society
  National Customs Service Association
  Organization of Professional Employees,
    Department of Agriculture
GENERAL UNIONS
  American Federation of Government Employees
  National Association of Government Employees
  National Federation of Federal Employees

The extent of unionization in the Executive
Branch varies considerably from organization to organization. The Post Office Department is the most thoroughly unionized; the two largest unions, the National
Association of Letter Carriers and the United Federation
of Postal Clerks, have 190,000 and 143,000 members
respectively. Scattered throughout the government, the
American Federation of Government Employees has
200,000 members. Approximately 165,000 federal workers belong to general government unions, and another
150,000 in the Tennessee Valley Authority, the Naval
Shipyards, the Government Printing Office, and other
industrial installations are in craft unions. To put these
figures in perspective, note that both the Teamsters and
the United Auto Workers have over a million members
and the Steelworkers over 900,000 members.

Like unions generally, government unions are interested in improving the well-being, especially the
material well-being, of their members. They are concerned about working conditions, appointments and
promotions, discipline, and of course pay and fringe

benefits. These concerns come out clearly in the hearings that Congress holds periodically to consider government pay bills. Union spokesmen come to argue the poverty of their condition and the need for improvement. The attendance of the union spokesmen at the hearings raises an important point. In matters of pay, public employee unions cannot bargain with management (as unions do in private business) because management can make no commitments. Pay raises come from Congress, and unions therefore go to Congress.[20] Because unions must bargain with Congress, and often with the President, the Civil Service Commission, and the Bureau of the Budget as well, it is obvious that they are politically active groups. A premium is placed on political activity, and skillful activity at that, because federal unions are forbidden to strike[21] by the Taft-Hartley Law as well as by their own constitutions. The unions thus cannot even threaten to strike; instead they must rely on bargaining, negotiation, political activity.

Unions do not deal only with Congress of course. They may also represent their members in dealing with agency management. Executive Order 10988, issued by President John F. Kennedy on January 17, 1962, elaborated and clarified this role of the union. In preparation for this order, President Kennedy appointed a Task Force on Employee Management Relations in the Federal Service and sent a memorandum setting up the Task Force to all heads of departments and agencies, stating his views on federal employee organizations.

> The fight of all employees of the federal government to join and participate in the activities of employee organizations and to seek to improve working conditions and the resolution of grievances should be recognized by management officials at all levels in all departments and agencies. The participation of federal

employees in the formulation and implementation of employee policies and procedures affecting them contributes to the effective conduct of public business.[22]

On November 30, 1961, the Task Force reported to the President, and its proposals were incorporated into Executive Order 10988. This order endorsed the prohibition of strikes, declared that closed and union shops were inappropriate, and indicated that conditions of employment fixed by Congress were not matters to be negotiated by labor and agency management. The order did make clear the employee's right to membership in an organization. The order delineated different forms of recognition that might be accorded employee organizations, and it set out the kinds of matters that were appropriate for labor management discussions—employee grievances, the work environment, and the scheduling of work are examples. In all, the order made clear that although there were limits on government unions, these organizations were legitimate and useful and should be recognized and used.

Many government employees are not unionized, and in some agencies (the Bureau of the Budget and the Department of State are two examples) practically none are. In addition, professional, technical, and administrative employees, like their counterparts in the business world, tend not to be unionized. But in two ways union activity and union successes affect these non-union employees. The pay raises that postal unions fight for reach men in other organizations eventually if not immediately. This is the more true since the 1962 Federal Salary Reform Act declared that under the different federal pay systems men doing equivalent work, even though in different organizations, should be paid at equal rates. But it is also true that the strength of the Postal unions (their membership is substantial and very wide-spread—in every Congressional district) and the political weakness of higher level professional and administrative employees results in a much narrower gap between bottom and top pay grades than is found in business and industry. One important reason for this lack of disparity is simply that low-level unionized employees have a louder voice than other employees.

One final point should be emphasized in this discussion of unions in the Executive Branch. Union entry into policy and politics is confined to employee welfare issues. Here they have substantial impact, perhaps more impact since Executive Order 10988 than ever before. But they do not participate in the full range of policies and programs that concern the Executive Branch. Their influence is important, but limited. In most policy areas they are irrelevant, and only in personnel matters is their relevance and impact obvious.

Notes for Chapter 3

1. This quotation is from page 30, Special Analyses, Budget of the United States, Fiscal Year 1967. See also Robert E. Hampton, "The Changing Federal Service," *Civil Service Journal*, April-June, 1964.

2. John J. Corson and R. Shale Paul, *Men Near the Top* (Baltimore: The Johns Hopkins Press, 1966), pp. 15–19.

3. The discussion will focus only on recruitment in the classified civil service and not directly consider recruitment in other federal personnel systems.

4. Frederick C. Mosher, "Features and Problems of the Federal Civil Service," in Wallace S. Sayre (ed.), *The Federal Government Service* (Englewood Cliffs, N.J.: Prentice-Hall, Inc., 1965), p. 174.

5. Employees in the classified civil service occupy one of eighteen ranks ranging from GS (General Schedule) 1 to GS 18, and each of these has several pay steps based largely on seniority. GS 1 thru 4 are grades normally occupied by clerical employees. An employee with a college degree normally starts his employment at GS-5 or GS-7, and an employee with a master's degree may start at GS-9. Grades 13, 14 and 15 are occupied by personnel with supervisory responsibilities and by professional employees. The last three grades are often called super grades; they are occupied by men with a high level of responsibility.

6. F. C. Mosher, *op. cit.*, p. 176.

7. "Personnel Management Research," United States Civil Service Commission, Washington, D.C., 1965, pp. 8–9.

8. Franklin P. Kilpatrick, Milton C. Cummings, Jr., and M. Kent Jennings, *The Image of the Federal Service* (Washington: The Brookings Institution, 1964), p. 117.

9. *Ibid.*, p. 124.

10. *Ibid.*, p. 140.

11. Richard F. Fenno, Jr., *The President's Cabinet* (New York: Random House, Vintage Books, 1959).

12. Dean E. Mann, *The Assistant Secretaries* (Washington: The Brookings Institution, 1965).

13. R. F. Fenno, *op. cit.*, chapter 2.

14. D. E. Mann, *op. cit.*, p. 76.

15. D. E. Mann, *op. cit.*, p. 264.

16. *The New York Times,* March 7, 1966, p. 1, reported that Schwartz had "been forced out" of his position. "Mr. Schwartz submitted to the White House last night his resignation as administrator of the Bureau of Security and Consular Affairs. He said it had been offered 24 hours after he learned that he was to be the principle victim of a reorganization to abolish

his bureau." According to the *Times* report, "Some high officials were too upset by the affair to discuss it. One described it as 'shabby'; another as 'scandalous.'" The reorganization and treatment of Schwartz ran into so much opposition that the reorganization plan was shelved rather than submitted to Congress for approval. According to the *Times* of June 19, 1966, p. 54 the resignation of Schwartz "set off a flurry of protest in liberal political circles and Congressman Henry Reuss and Senator Robert Kennedy both promised investigations when the reorganization proposal was submitted by the President to the Congress." The plan was not submitted that year.

17. U. S. Civil Service Commission, *Federal Personnel Manual*, Civil Service Rule IV, Sec. 04.1, quoted in O. Glenn Stahl, *Public Personnel Administration*, 5th ed. (New York: Harper and Row, 1962), p. 367.

18. *Report of the Commission on Political Activity of Government Personnel*, vol. 1 (Washington, 1968), p. 20.

19. *Ibid.*, p. 21.

20. Legislation passed in 1912 authorized federal employees to organize and petition Congress both individually and collectively.

21. Stahl makes a relevant point: "The general rule in the United States is that what a civil servant is not permitted to do as an individual, he may not do by indirection as a member of an association. Thus, organization of public employees or their representatives, even when such representatives are not themselves civil servants, are often barred from political activity. In practice, however, it has proved much more difficult to control such organizational activity than that of individuals, and public employee organizations have in fact engaged in political activity to further the ends of their membership." *op. cit.*, p. 369.

22. Quoted in Chester A. Newland, "Trends in Public Employee Unionization," *Journal of Politics*, vol. 26 (1964), p. 588.

UNDERSTANDING
THE ORGANIZATIONS

THE EXECUTIVE BRANCH is made up of formal organizations—more specifically, of bureaucratic organizations.[1] This chapter reviews some of what is known about the characteristics of such organizations and the behavior of the people in them. The assumption is that some knowledge of these matters is helpful and perhaps indispensable in trying to understand the Executive Branch. For example, to appreciate the difficulties that a Cabinet member may face in controlling his department, it seems useful to know something about organizational communications, status systems, authority systems, and incentive systems; and it may be useful to be able

Notes for this chapter appear on pages 117–120.

to view a department as a political system in which the Secretary must share power with others. In general, many of the concepts introduced in this chapter should help the student to understand the Executive Branch as a part of the political system.

What Is a Formal Organization?

Theodore Caplow has written: "An organization is a social system that has an unequivocal collective identity, an exact roster of members, a program of activity, and procedures for replacing members."[2] It is obvious that organizations in the Executive Branch fit this definition. Introducing their book on formal organizations, Peter Blau and W. Richard Scott say: "This book is about organizations—organizations of various kinds, with diverse aims, of varying size and complexity, and with different characteristics. What they all have in common is that a number of men have become organized into a social unit—an organization—that has been established for the explicit purpose of achieving certain goals."[3] The organizations of the Executive Branch would seem to fit this definition. To be sure, the clarity of their goals is often open to question, but that the organizations are established to accomplish certain goals is indisputable. One of the common phrases in the Executive Branch is, "Our mission is to . . . ."

Edgar Schein, in his valuable little book, *Organizational Psychology*,[4] defines organization as follows:

> An organization is a rational coordination of the activities of a number of people for the achievement of some common explicit purpose or goal, through division of labor and function, and through a hierarchy of authority and responsibility.

This definition overlaps the previous definitions, but it also introduces new ideas—division of labor and hierarchy. Schein's definition thus moves us from formal organization to bureaucratic organization. In the literature on organizations there is some confusion in the use of these two terms, but we may let the definitions of Caplow and Blau and Scott fit formal organizations and the definition of Schein fit bureaucratic organizations.

The organizations in the Executive Branch are not only formal organizations but also bureaucratic organizations. Any government agency, with its divisions, sections, and offices (Personnel Office, Budget Office, Data Processing Division) clearly exhibits division of labor and specialization. Hierarchy is also clear. A common bureaucratic phrase is "chain of command," and the chain runs (on paper!) from the President through the Secretary and Bureau Chief down to the most junior employee. Although it is risky, it is common to think of bureaucratic organizations as pyramids of authority, with one man at the pinnacle and many men at the bottom. It is risky simply because the man at the top is not the only one with authority; the men in the middle and indeed the ones at the bottom possess it also.

The process of defining "formal organization" and "bureaucratic organization" is really an exercise in listing the characteristics of such organizations. In effect we are saying that people in groups exhibiting particular characteristics are members of bureaucratic organizations. Max Weber, a nineteenth century German sociologist, provided a famous list of bureaucratic characteristics, and future writers have added to it, modified it, and changed the wording. An article[5] that appeared a few years ago drew on the work of a number of scholars and provided the following list of bureaucratic characteristics:

Hierarchy of authority

Division of labor

Technically competent participants

Procedural devices for work situations

Rules governing behavior of positional incumbents

Limited authority of office

Differential rewards by office

Impersonality of personal contact

Administration separate from ownership

Emphasis on written communications

Rational discipline

Not all writers point to all of these and, more important, not all organizations exhibit these characteristics to the same degree. In fact it is useful to think of each of these characteristics as existing on a continuum running from more to less; bureaucratization itself may be a matter of degree. Research along these lines has concentrated on nongovernment organizations, but it is certainly a plausible hypothesis that not all government organizations are equally bureaucratic. Some organizations may be less impersonal than others; some may have a much more developed division of labor than others; some may rely much more than others on technically competent participants.

It is important to bear in mind that nothing in the definition or characterization of bureaucracy implies that bureaucratic organizations are found only in the public government context. Name virtually any industrial corporation—American Telephone and Telegraph, General Motors, U.S. Steel, Sears and Roebuck—and you have named a bureaucratic organization. Among numerous other examples is the Roman Catholic Church. Many of the charges that are often leveled at government bureaucratic organizations can be leveled at other organizations as well.

Several perspectives, several ways of thinking about organizations, are helpful in trying to understand how organizations operate and why they operate the way they do. A bureaucratic organization is first of all a *social system*. Organizations are systems of *authority* and *status*, they can be viewed as *political systems*. Organizations can be viewed as *communication networks* with many senders and receivers of messages, and organizations have been described as *economies of incentives*. Organizations are both *formal* and *informal;* that is, they have both formal and informal aspects. And finally, for any organization, there is both an *image* and a *reality*. There may be a performance on stage intended to be seen; inevitably there is also action and inaction back stage, not intended for the public.[6] These perspectives may aid us in understanding the Executive Branch and the behavior of bureaucrats and bureaucratic organizations.

Bureaucratic Organizations as Social Systems

What does it mean to say that an organization is a social system? In defining an organization as a social system Theodore Caplow begins with this definition:[7]

> A *social system* is a set of persons with an identifying characteristic plus a set of relationships established among these persons by interaction. As in other fields of analysis, in order to describe a system we must be able to identify all the elements that belong in the system and exclude all those that do not belong. We

must be able to use consistent criteria to do this. In a social system, we must be able to identify the persons involved—which means that they must have at least one distinctive characteristic in common—and must also be able to show that these people are related by interaction.

Not all sociologists use the same language, but Caplow's definition would doubtless be accepted by many. To put it more simply, a social system is an identifiable group of people who interact with one another.

In trying to understand bureaucratic organizations it is important to have in mind the properties of social systems. First, a social system contains many different positions and roles which are filled by the members of the organization. In addition it may also be characterized by subgroups or subsystems. A social system exhibits norms and values and has sanctions to enforce them. And, finally, all social systems share common problems.

A glance at the organization chart or personnel roster of any organization will confirm that social systems contain different positions. A corollary consistent with the hierarchical structure of bureaucratic organizations is that there are varied numbers of different positions. The Federal Bureau of Investigation has one Director, several Assistant Directors, many Special Agents in Charge of Field Offices, and very many Special Agents. There are also, of course, secretaries, chemists, photographers, and many other positions, displaying not only hierarchical structure but also specialization and division of labor. Other government organizations also exhibit a more or less complex position structure; the larger the number of different activities carried on by the organization, the greater will be the variety of positions in the organization.

In addition to positions a social system has roles

which the members of the organization fill or play. The distinction between position and role is often not easy to understand, but it is worth making. A position amounts to a more or less detailed prescription of the behavior required of a particular organization member. A role is what the member of the organization actually does. Now it may seem at first that organization position and organization role are two names for the same thing, but this is not necessarily the case. A role—that is, actual performance—is affected by the formal position prescription, but only partly. A role is also affected by the informal and unwritten expectations and desires of other organization members and perhaps in some circumstances nonmembers as well; performance is also the result of a member's interpretation of the written prescription and his own ability and willingness to do what is prescribed. Because performance is affected by so many variables, it is hazardous to assume that organization members are actually doing what their formal position descriptions say they ought to be doing. Position descriptions may have more to do with wished-for than real behavior. In real life men in identical positions may be doing very different things. A man who steps into another's position may fill it differently; no man in an organization may quite live up to the formal prescription of his position.

In addition to positions and roles a social system may have subgroups or subsystems. In Executive Branch organizations this is obvious; departments have bureaus and offices, and they in turn have divisions and sections. Even within a relatively small group there may be subsystems, called by many "cliques" or "informal work groups." The existence of subgroups is important because they may have norms, values, and sanctions which are separate from and perhaps in conflict with the values of the whole system. The Office of the Secretary of Defense, for example, may have goals and values that are its alone and not shared by other components of the Defense Department—the Department of the Army, the Navy, and the Air Force—and they in turn differ from each other. Whether a group is a system or a subsystem depends, of course, on one's perspective. A Cabinet department can be viewed as a system and its components as subsystems. But from another point of view the same department is a subsystem of the Executive Branch —which itself is part of the American political system.

What does it mean to say that a social system has norms and values? In brief the members of a social system expect all its members to act or behave in particular ways. Norms can be thought of as informal and unwritten rules and can be distinguished from the written rules of an organization. The relationship between the written rules and informal norms is by no means simple. The content of the written rules and informal norms may be the same, and the two may reinforce each other. There may be norms, but no rules, regulating some kinds of behavior. There may, for example, be no written rules regulating contact between organizational members and newspaper reporters, but the norm may be that employees do not talk to members of the press. Written rules and norms may conflict with one another; the rule may be that employees report for work at 8:00 A.M.; but organizational norms may permit arriving at any time between 8:00 A.M. and 9:00 A.M. Because both norms and written rules influence behavior and do not necessarily reinforce one another, it is hazardous to predict individual behavior on the basis of a knowledge of only the written rules. It is therefore unwise to assume that organization members are behaving in ways consistent with the formal regulations simply because the regulations exist. Promulgating a new regulation may have little or no effect on behavior, especially if the norm is to ignore formalities. One implication is that if an executive or a Congressman or a citizen wants to know what government employees are doing he needs indicators more reliable than the regulations. He needs accurate information about informal norms and, best of all, information on actual behavior.

Norms are guides to conduct, and every social system has them. Not all norms will apply equally to every position or role in an organization nor to every subsystem. Norms (or expectations) that apply to the Chief may not apply to subordinate employees, and of course the reverse may also be true. Within a system, in other words, there may be role-specific norms. It would be a plausible hypothesis that the more isolated a subsystem is from the total system the more likely it is to have subsystem-specific norms and the less likely it is to share all the total system norms. The norms that apply in one field office may not apply in another.

Why do norms exist? There is no single simple answer to this question. One general reason is that they function to ease interaction among the members of a system or subsystem. Norms may result in predictable, stable behavior and amicable relations. Norms exist to make being together more endurable. They may serve to limit conflict and encourage cooperation. More generally organizational norms may help an organization meet its goals. It would be a mistake, however, to try to explain the norms or values found in an organization on rational grounds alone. Given the emotional and nonrational content of individual behavior, nonrational norms should be expected. For example, there may be an expectation (a norm) that a promotion to section chief brings a larger desk and a promotion to division chief brings a wooden (instead of metal) desk. More senior personnel may also be allowed more discretion in their use of time; they may be allowed to come and go at will. Not to honor such an organizational norm may lower job satisfaction and productivity and increase conflict within the organization. What to an outsider may appear to make no sense at all may be an accepted part of organizational life—and to ignore or attempt to alter it may be disruptive. To be sure, it may be costly to follow organizational norms, but it may be costly not to. The costs of both courses need to be assessed before either is chosen.

Norms and written rules would mean little if there were not also sanctions, both positive and negative, to insure compliance. Written rules may be accompanied by a system of formal discipline, but there may also be informal sanctions. Members of an organization may be rewarded for conforming to organizational norms with everything from acceptance, respect, and friendship to choice assignments, promotions, and more money. The executive who conforms to the norms of an organization, who fits in, may be rewarded with loyalty; he will be a leader who is followed. The executive who ignores the norms of an organization may be rewarded with mutiny and its modern-day equivalents. Negative sanctions have to be reckoned with by any member of a social system. Obviously the senior members of a social system control some sanctions; they can use the formal discipline system to get rules obeyed. But junior members also have their sanctions. By slowing down, by striking, by sabotaging, junior members can make their displeasure known. It is a naïve executive who thinks his subordinates have no control over him. In fact the superior-subordinate relationship is a relationship of mutual accommodation. Either party, if he moves too far too fast from what is normal, may be sanctioned in some way.

To complete this brief discussion of social systems some attention must be given to their common problems. Organizations have the problem of maintaining themselves, and this fundamental problem implies several more. There is the problem of recruiting and retaining members; and these members must be socialized, trained, and rewarded. Surely it is clear that success or failure in dealing with these tasks may have dramatic effect on the organization. Next, internal conflict must be limited and cooperation maintained. The organization must be integrated. The problem of integration or cohesion is faced by every social system, and when it is not dealt with successfully the system dissolves. It should be emphasized that the threat of disintegration is always present in an organization that has many members and subsystems.

To endure, an organization must be able to respond to its environment; this is particularly important when the continuance of an organization depends on its responding to demands originating outside the organization. To respond to its environment an organization must be able to define the relevant environment and to communicate with it. Here again the process of mutual adjustment is important. An organization that isolates itself and does not communicate with its environment may perish, but an organization that can and does respond to its environment may gain attention and support. By communicating what it can do (public information and education) to the environment (the public), an organization may be able to meet the demands that are made on it. A final common problem faced by any organization is goal definition. Why does the organization exist? What is it trying to do? Or, in government language, what is its mission? Failure to deal with this question may result in scattered use of resources, inability to define the relevant environment, and eventual disintegration.

Authority in Organizations

Organizations are composed of members with varying amounts of authority concerning different matters, and the authority of members rests on varying bases. We have already seen that bureaucratic organizations appear to resemble a pyramid of authority, a chain of command. The chief of an organization, the man at the pinnacle of the pyramid, ordinarily has more authority than any other man in the organization. But his deputies and assistants, the men in middle management, and indeed men far down the hierarchy also have authority. The President of the United States shares authority with White House staff members, department Secretaries and bureau chiefs, and the heads of independent agencies. And these men in turn share authority with their subordinates.

Why does a chief executive share authority? Some men in the organization may in some matters have more expertise, and their knowledge gives them authority. Some men may have more seniority or experience; others may have more time. An executive pressed for time may share his authority with an assistant and delegate to him authority over some matters to lighten his own workload. Authority may be shared as a training technique to prepare a subordinate to become a chief executive. It may be shared unavoidably with a man who has the support of other organization members or outsiders, which suggests that authority-sharing may be a political tactic used to gain support or to spread responsibility. All these reasons (and the list is hardly exhaustive) emphasize that authority-sharing is inevitable in a formal organization.

The authority of organization members varies in at least two dimensions. One of these is a finality dimension. As Kaufman has pointed out, a forest ranger has final authority in very few matters; most of his decisions have to go to regional or national headquarters for review before they become final.[8] The further down in the hierarchy a man is, generally the more limited are the matters over which he has final authority. The further up he is the more extended is his range of final authority. There is also a breadth or scope dimension. In understanding this notion it will pay to remember the bureaucratic characteristics of specialization and division of labor. Budget officers and personnel officers have authority of limited scope. Within that scope their authority may be final, but the scope is narrow. The authority of a division chief is limited commonly to his division, and even the authority of an assistant secretary in a department may be limited to some particular area of organizational activity. The chief of an organization of course has the widest scope of authority, at least in form.

In trying to understand any organization, it is useful to ask "Who has authority over what?" but it must be remembered that the answer will not necessarily be found in the organization charts and manuals. Authority is as much a matter of informal acceptance as it is a matter of formal prescription, and to find out who has it one must ask questions and actually observe. A man with formal authority in a technical or scientific organization may be technically ignorant and as a result have little authority. A young chief executive may find that he has little authority over the organization's senior members. A man so far down in an organization that he appears on no charts may be able to influence the behavior of his fellows with a few words. Such are the complexities of trying to describe or explain authority in organizations. In fact, to understand the authority system of any organization it is necessary not only to look at the formal organization but also to study the power structure.

The Organization as a Political System

To consider the subject of authority in organizations is to make clear why an organization is a political system.[9] Whenever the distribution of authority is involved, political behavior is present. Political behavior involves conflict and conflict resolution. It involves negotiation and bargaining and coalition building. All these activities go on inside bureaucratic organizations. The political-system perspective emphasizes that, though an organization may have leaders and followers, the followers commonly constrain the leaders. As in any political system, leaders need support (and productivity) from their followers; and to get it they must meet at least some of the demands of some of their followers some of the time. The leader-follower relationship is one of mutual adjustment.

Just as there are varying kinds of national political systems, so are there varying kinds of organizational political systems. A research laboratory staffed largely with Ph.D.'s might at one extreme exhibit little hierarchy, few rules, and much freedom and equality. The National Bureau of Standards has been called "the campus." A police organization (perhaps the FBI is an example) may have much less freedom, the emphasis on hierarchy may be much more marked, and there may be many more rules to be rigidly adhered to. Just as among national states, there are varying degrees of absoluteness among organizations.

Incentives in an Organization

The authority perspective asks, "Who has authority over whom or what?" The incentive perspective asks "Who has how many and what kinds of incentives or resources at his disposal?" (It would not be particularly surprising if in any single organization the answer to both these questions was the same.) Several related questions can be raised. What are incentives used for? What kinds of incentives may be available in an organization? Who controls the distribution of what incentives? These questions have been dealt with most clearly in a chapter in Chester Barnard's classic book, *The Functions of the Executive*,[10] and in an article by Peter Clark and James Wilson, "Incentive Systems: A Theory of Organizations."[11]

Most generally, incentives are used to elicit contributions to the organization from members of the organization. What kind of contributions? Contributions of time, energy, skill, thought, loyalty—all essential inputs if an organization is to survive and prosper. What can be used to elicit such contributions? An obvious answer is money, but it is only one of the several material incentives that an organization may use. Organizations may also provide cars, housing, personal assistance, insurance, medical care, and so on. In addition to material incentives organizations have nonmaterial incentives or rewards that, like material rewards, may be given or withheld. Free time and discretion in the use of time may be desired by some organizational members. The opportunity to participate in decision-making may serve as an incentive. The opportunity to mix socially with superiors or influential clients may be valued. The goals of an organization itself (keeping the world safe, helping the less fortunate) may serve as an incentive.

Several qualifications and complications should be kept in mind when thinking about incentives. One is that there are limits on the use of money as an incentive. Members of an organization may value other things more highly—more free time, more leisure. Virtually any incentive, including money, may have a point of diminishing returns. This point may differ for different members of an organization, but that does not alter the basic proposition. As a man's salary goes higher and higher, additional increments of money may prove to be less powerful incentives. Other incentives have their limits too, of course, but it is especially important to emphasize the limitations of money as an incentive because it is so commonly used in American society.

Because no organization has an unlimited stock of incentives or resources at its disposal, it must budget its resources and use them effectively. There is little point in using money as an incentive in situations where it is likely not to be effective, or to accomplish what a little leisure or some other incentive might accomplish better. Within limits incentives may substitute for each other. An executive needs to be clear about what incentives he has at his disposal and what each is good for.

Just as men's needs vary, so too do the incentives that will move them. The mix of pay, fringe benefits, vacations, and holidays that excites one man may not excite another. In terms of individual contributions, individually tailored incentive schemes might be most productive, but they might also be too costly for an organization. This point brings up another: that what an individual wants an organization may not be able to provide. It may not be within the power of an organization to offer what will move some men. As a result, they don't become members of an organization, or they leave, or they stay but don't contribute. We have seen already that many professionals do not think federal service offers what they want in a job, and we have seen also that federal executives leave because they can make more money elsewhere.

Incentives may have a diminishing effect. Rewards may become expected, *pro forma,* and lose their force. Not to receive what he expects may lessen a member's contribution, but to receive only what he thinks he is owed may not increase his contribution. Indeed, if a member does not gradually receive more, his contribution may lessen. Just to maintain a man's contribution may require that his rewards from the organization gradually increase. To increase the contribution from him may require an even steeper increase in his rewards.

Everything said so far suggests that an organization needs a substantial supply of varied incentives if it is to be able easily to attract and keep members and induce substantial contributions of their time and energy. Of course organizations vary in the quantity and variety of their incentives and thus vary in their attractiveness to members and potential members. An apparent shortage of incentives need not be disabling; if an organization is able to offer the incentives that its members want, then it needs no more. But when incentives available and incentives demanded are not congruent then clearly an organization is in trouble.

Before the subject of incentives is closed, one more question must be raised. Who controls the distribution of incentives? Ordinarily the control of incentives is closely related to the hierarchy of authority. How could an executive influence behavior if he did not control incentives? But there are qualifications to this control. A standard complaint in public administration is that government executives have responsibility but no authority. A more meaningful complaint might be that executives have both authority and responsibility but little control over the distribution of incentives. In the Executive Branch the distribution of both material and nonmaterial incentives is controlled to a great extent by Congressional legislation and Civil Service Commission rules. An executive or supervisor is not free to reward whom he chooses how he chooses. This prevents favoritism, which is the intention, but it may also limit what an executive can do to obtain contributions from his subordinates.

It should also be kept in mind that it may be in the power of many members of the organization to distribute nonmaterial incentives or rewards. Friendship, respect, or acceptance may be granted or withheld by individuals and subsystems throughout an organization. A man may want these as much as he wants the pay and promotions controlled by the hierarchical authorities. The hierarchy may indeed find that it has little influence; and if the goals of the work groups diverge from the goals of the hierarchy, the goals of the hierarchy may not be met.

What these comments suggest is that in any organization there are both a formal and an informal incentive system. The formal incentives are officially recognized, and their distribution is controlled by the hierarchical authorities. Informal incentives are not officially recognized, their distribution is controlled by informal leaders, and officials may not be aware of their existence. These two systems may reinforce one another or may conflict. If they reinforce one another, then the members can be expected to contribute what the organization requires, and the goals of the organization will be met. If they conflict, the organization may not obtain the contributions it requires to meet its goals. These remarks should not be taken to mean that hierarchical leaders may not also distribute informal incentives; they may arrange to be photographed with a subordinate or praise him publicly or wink at rule violations. But again the point is that what the hierarchical leaders have to offer may not be able to compete successfully with what others have to offer.

Status in Organizations

The members of a bureaucratic organization have different amounts of status; there are high-status members, low-status members and men in the middle. Status is a summary word that is related to rights, freedoms, discretion, respect. Rather than saying that a man has higher rank, more rights, more discretion and enjoys more respect than others, we simply say that he has more or higher status.

Status is important in organizations because increments in status may serve as incentives, and the symbols associated with status may serve as incentives. The private office, the larger office, the wooden desk, the private secretary, the phone extension, the rug, the fireplace —all these are the accoutrements of bureaucratic status. In a status-conscious bureaucracy a larger desk may have the same effect as a raise, and the larger office that comes with a promotion may be as important as the promotion itself. The astute executive knows the status symbols in his organization (he may even popularize a few) and often uses them as incentives. Status symbols, besides acting as incentives, serve a completely different function. They legitimate the communications that pass back and forth in the organization. In the army, insignia of rank make it clear who may give orders and who must obey them. In civilian organizations, too, the symbols of office make it clear whose words must be listened to. Status symbols tell those who see them that the person displaying them "is someone."

A status system is useful (and indeed inevitable), but there are costs associated with a status system. It may lead to inflexibility and be an obstacle to innovation. The observations and ideas of men of relatively low status may be undervalued (perhaps ignored) and the ideas and opinions of men with relatively high status may be overvalued. Men with high status are likely to want to preserve it and thus may resist any changes that might alter their status. People who are well off may want to continue their condition. Even if a chief executive sees a need to reorganize, he may resist doing so if the changes would effect the status of personnel; he may realize that such changes would be opposed and even if successful might lower morale and productivity and increase turnover. When status is involved executives have to move cautiously and may occasionally try to maintain a man's status even while downgrading his responsibilities.

What are the bases of status in an organization? Organizational status tends to follow social status. But there are other bases too. The position in the hierarchy that an occupational member occupies obviously affects his status. The difficulty of the task done by an organizational member affects his status. In other words the amount of skill that a job requires affects the status of the person doing it. How rare the skill and of course how important the work to the organization is relevant.

The Organization as Communication Network

To the several perspectives so far discussed we can add another—communications. This perspective suggests several questions that can help us understand Executive Branch organizations. The most general question (it is really several questions) is: Who communicates with whom how frequently about what and with what effect? This question implies a useful model of the communications process in formal organizations.

Every member of an organization can be viewed as a communicator or potential communicator of information. But all these communicators do not communicate with everyone else in the organization. If they did, the organization would be Babel. Instead each communicator communicates with a defined and usually limited number of others. (Each sender of messages has only a defined and limited number of receivers.) Formal communication is likely to be controlled by rules that specify who should be contacted or informed about what. A low-level employee may do little more than communicate with fellow employees and his immediate superior, and any communication he has with more senior persons in the organization is likely to be indirect and carried out by his superior. A superior has contact with his subordinates, with his peers, and with his superior. He may also have contact with a personnel officer, a budget officer, and other representatives of higher echelons in the organization. A bureau chief will have contact with his deputy and his assistants and with the heads of divisions and offices. His name is likely to appear on general orders that go to everyone in his organization. He will have contact with departmental officials and some other bureau chiefs. In general, the more senior a person is in his organization, the more widespread are his formal communications. The more complex his responsibilities, the more people from whom he must get information and the more to whom he must give information.

The reverse of the statement that everyone is a potential communicator is that everyone in an organization is a potential receiver. And just as communication is limited, so is formal or official reception limited. Formally a man can be expected to receive the information he needs to do his job, he may receive little or much information. But in practice it is often extremely difficult, if not impossible, to specify what a man needs to know to do his job. A man may be flooded with information and unable to pay attention to what is necessary, or he may suffer from a dearth of information. In the name of protecting him, his subordinates may prevent him from getting data he needs.

There is an additional communications role in any organization—the role of relay. Bureau chiefs issue orders that are transmitted through assistants and middle management down to front-line supervisors and the men. Employees ask questions and register complaints and send reports that may go through several levels. The interaction of the relay, the communicator, and the receiver can have substantial consequences for an organization. Consider only the difference in effect between a message that is intelligible, is relayed accurately, and is clearly received, and a message that is intelligible originally but is inaccurately relayed, and is thus incorrectly received. Messages that are originally unintelligible can be sent also, and intelligible messages sent and relayed accurately can still be received unclearly.

The impact that the relay may have on the content of communications should not be underestimated. To be sure, the relay is usually expected to do nothing but receive a message and send it on its way as automatically as a TV relay. The human relay, however, may be a source of misinterpretation, distortion, and inaccurate repeating. Indeed, a relay may send on a message that was not sent originally. Anyone who doubts this and does not want to read the literature on serial communications can simply play the parlor game of sending an oral message around a circle of adults and listening to what comes out. Imagine what can happen as reports and memoranda get condensed, and condensed, and condensed, until finally they land on the Secretary's or the President's desk.

It may have appeared thus far as though communication within organizations were only formal, but of course it is not. In any organization there is informal but nevertheless functional communication, ranging from the informal oral agreement that precedes a formal written exchange to informal checking with subordinates before formally issuing an order. This kind of informal (perhaps spontaneous is a better word) communication occurs because organization communication rules ordinarily do not and probably could not cover all situations which may require communication.

In any organization there will also be informal social communication. Such communication may appear to have nothing whatever to do with the job at hand— except insofar as respite from a job may be necessary to continued performance of the job. But it may be that social communication supports the communication channels that are also used for formal communication. It may be that ability to communicate socially with someone enhances ability to communicate formally with him about the job.

How frequently do communications take place? The easy answer is that it depends. An organization's communications rules may specify that some communications take place on a regular basis; reports will be submitted weekly or daily, semi-annually or monthly. Some communications may take place not regularly but only when specified conditions are met or when particular problems arise. In other words, communication may be both routine and *ad hoc*. The scope of authority and the specialization of an organization member will affect both how frequently he receives messages and how frequently he sends them. Location also affects frequency of communication. Communication with the person in the next office may be constant; communication with a man across the country may be less frequent. Communication technology is also important, as is cost; when long-distance telephone rates go down, the number of calls goes up. The analyst of communications may be interested in two questions dealing with frequency: (1) How frequently are particular types of messages sent? and (2) How frequently do particular organization members send and/or receive messages?

What effect do communications have? In considering this question it should be remembered that not all communications are intended to produce action. Surely this is true of much social communication; it can also be true of formal communication. Much formal communication is intended only to inform, not to get action. (Military communications may go to two sets of receivers—action addressees, who are supposed to respond to the message, and information addressees, who presumably are expected only to read the message.) However, much communication within an organization is intended to get action. Does it? It may, but it may not. Richard Neustadt, in his book, *Presidential Power*,[12] discusses the factors that encourage compliance with Presidential orders, or in other language, positive response to Presidential communications.

> The first factor favoring compliance with a Presidential order is assurance that the President has spoken.

> A second factor making for compliance with a President's request is clarity about his meaning.

> A third factor favoring compliance with a President's directive is publicity.

> A fourth factor favoring compliance with a President's request is actual ability to carry it out.

> A fifth factor making for compliance with a President's request is the sense that what he wants is his by right.

Neustadt's observations are relevant to the communications sent by any chief executive in an organization. If these conditions are not met, communications may have little effect; orders may flow but nothing will happen.

A final concept should be mentioned in this discussion of communication—information overload. In brief, this means that a man can be deluged with more information than he can receive and understand. When this happens, messages sent are, in effect, not received. Because the consequences can be serious (imagine the possible consequences of the Secretary of Defense not being aware that U.S. reconnaissance planes were flying over Communist China or not being aware that one had just been shot down), organizations and executives take steps to avoid overload. (Sometimes they don't succeed; sometimes they don't try.) Delegation, authority-sharing, specialization, and division of labor have been mentioned already and are relevant here. Priority codes—*routine, priority, critical*—may be placed on each communication to ensure that the most important messages get through. (There remains the problem of how to code any particular message.) Visitors are screened, and messages are filtered and condensed by subordinates to save their superior's time. All such steps are useful, but the resultant danger is that because of such protection an executive will not know what he needs to know. Information overload is a real danger in the twentieth century, but ignorance also poses a constant threat. Devising organizational communications systems that skirt both dangers is a constant challenge.

Individuals in Organizations

"This book is about the organization man." So begins a famous book, *The Organization Man*. The author, William H. Whyte, describes the subject of his book this way:[13]

> If the term is vague, it is because I can think of no other way to describe the people I am talking about. They are not the workers, nor are they the white collar people in the usual, clerk sense of the word. These people only work for The Organization. The ones I am talking about *belong* to it as well. They are the ones of our middle class who have left home, spiritually as well as physically, to take the vows of organization life, and it is they who are the mind and soul of our great self-perpetuating institutions.

With such language Whyte describes one pattern of adjustment to work in bureaucratic organizations. It would be a mistake, however, to think that it is the only pattern; many social scientists have looked inside organizations and used a variety of terms to describe the various behavior patterns they have found.

In a popular book written some years after Whyte's, Robert Presthus divided organizational members into three types—the upward mobiles, the ambivalents, and the indifferents.[14]

> The upward mobiles are typically distinguished by high morale; their level of job satisfaction is high. Indeed, the process and criteria by which they are selected insures that they will have an unfailing optimism. The reasons for this are clear. They identify strongly with the organization and derive strength from their involvement. Their dividends also include disproportionate shares of the organization's rewards in power, income, and ego reinforcement.

Unlike the upward mobiles, the indifferents, according to Presthus, do not identify with the organization. "The indifferents are those who have come to terms with their *work environment* by withdrawal and by a redirection of their interests toward off-the-job satisfactions."[15] Further, Presthus wrote, "The typical indifferent has rejected majority values of success and power. While the upward mobile strives for such values, obtainable today mainly through big organizations, the indifferent seeks that security which the organization can also provide for those who merely go 'along'."[16]

In the middle, between the upward mobiles and the indifferents, are the ambivalents. The ambivalent wants the prizes or rewards given by the organization, but he does not, as it were, want to play the game to get them. Perhaps he cannot. Presthus writes:[17]

> On the one hand, he wants success yet resists paying the price in collectively validated behavior. On the

other, he disdains success, as popularly defined, yet feels that his individuality must be validated by others. Unable to reject or to rise above majority values, he is also unable or unwilling to play the roles required to achieve them. While the upward mobile is sustained by status rewards and great expectations, and the indifferent accommodates by limiting his aspirations, the ambivalent is chronically disturbed.

Presthus ascribes to the ambivalent, despite his seeming confusion, an important organizational role, that of critic and innovator.[18]

Despite his inability to meet bureaucratic demands, the ambivalent type plays a critical social role, namely, that of providing the insight, motivation, and dialectic that inspire change. His innovating role is often obscured because the authority, leadership, and money needed to institutionalize change remain in the hands of organizational elites. Nevertheless, few ideals or institutions escape his critical scrutiny. In his view custom is no guarantee of either rationality or legitimacy. This perception is sharpened by his inability to accept charismatic and traditional bases of authority: rationality alone provides a compelling standard.

The concepts "cosmopolitan" and "local" also help us understand how individuals may adjust to work in a bureaucratic organization. These words have been used by several scholars to describe organization members who identify with the organization in which they work (locals) and organization members who identify with some external group (cosmopolitans). This dichotomy, of course, is not unlike the trichotomy proposed by Presthus.[19] "In the context of Merton's distinction, the upward mobile is typically a 'local.' Unlike the 'cosmopolitan' who has a broad disciplinary interest or national perspective, his interests and aspirations are tied to his own organization. Always loyal, he regards its rules and actions as 'the one best way' to handle large numbers of people." If the local and the upward mobile can be equated, so perhaps can the ambivalent and the cosmopolitan. Gouldner has described the cosmopolitan as low on loyalty to the employing organization, likely to use an external reference group, and high on commitment to professional skills.[20] The ambivalent has been described in similar language.[21] "He honors theory, knowledge, and skill. Socialization as an independent professional blinds him to legitimate, organizational needs for control and coordination. Believing explicitly that both motivation and expertise come from within he resists bureaucratic rules and supervision."

Other studies, using other langauge, have focused on similar patterns of adaption. Leonard Reissman's "Role Conceptions in Bureaucracy," for example, set out to determine what the civil servant conceived his social role to be.[22] In data he collected in a state civil service Reissman found four ideal types of role conception.

1. Functional bureaucrat—seeks recognition from professional group outside of bureaucracy—just happens to work for the government—faces outward and away from the bureaucracy—active in professional societies—guided by standards of success of the profession.

2. Specialist bureaucrat—resembles functional bureaucrat but more aware of bureaucracy—seeks recognition from department and people with whom he works—overly meticulous about the rules and regulations, he attempts always to remain safely within these limits.

3. Service bureaucrat—oriented in terms of bureaucratic structure but seeks recognition from outside group.

    4. Job bureaucrat—immersed entirely in structure—
seeks recognition along departmental rather than
professional lines—improvement of operating efficiency becomes an end in itself.

These four patterns of adaptation are similar to the
three types of adaptation proposed by Marvick in his
Career Perspectives in a Bureaucratic Setting[23] and to
those found by Slesinger in his *Personnel Adaptations in
the Federal Junior Management Assistant Program.*[24]
Marvick, analyzing data collected in a government research organization, found what he called institutional-
ists, specialists, and hybrids. As defined by him these
different patterns of career identification resemble the
job bureaucrat, the functional bureaucrat, and the specialist bureaucrat that Reissman described. (Marvick
did not distinguish a service bureaucrat.) The cosmopolitan and the local, the specialist and institutionalist,
the functional bureaucrat and the job bureaucrat are different terms that describe the same dichotomy: weak
identification with the employing organization and
strong identification with it. But having mentioned this
it may be more accurate to view organizational identification as existing on a continuum with the ends marked
strong and weak.

    Another aspect of individual behavior within bu-
reaucratic organizations can be clearly if inelegantly
described as "rule-following behavior." This behavior
can be viewed as a continuum running from "always
obeys the rules" to "seldom obeys the rules." Presthus
noted that the ambivalent resisted bureaucratic rules
and supervision while the upward mobile accepted them.
Reissman suggested that the specialist bureaucrat was
"overly meticulous about rules and regulations." An
article which appeared some years ago described how

different Navy disbursing officers adjusted to rules.[25] "The Regulation type approximates the true bureaucrat in that he remains impervious to rank, informal structures, and the orders of his superiors, but goes further in employing the narrowest possible interpretation of every regulation. For fear of the General Accounting Office his rule is, "When in doubt, don't."[26] Officers described as realists, on the other hand, saw the regulations "as illogical concatenations of procedures, restrictions, and interpretations, frequently ambiguous, sometimes contradictory, and often, when strictly applied, defeating the purpose for which they were constructed."[27]

Some, but not necessarily all, organization members will resemble the model of the archetypal bureaucrat described so well by Merton in his classic "Bureaucratic Structure and Personality."[28] Surely some may conscientiously obey and enforce every single rule no matter what the situation or consequences, but not all will. Moreover, whether a person obeys the rules may not necessarily depend on the strength of his identification with his organization. An upward mobile, for example, may pay little attention to formal rules and regulations if such behavior is the norm in his organization. If one knew only that a man was strongly identified with his organization, it would be unsafe to predict his rule-following behavior. It would be safe to predict only that he would conform to the norms of his organization.

A little imagination can produce more labels to describe the ways in which organization members have adapted to the various demands of organizational life.[29] The *more involved* and the *less involved* or, much less neutrally, *stakhonovite* and *slacker* are terms that could be used to describe, respectively, the members who work 12 hours a day and on nights and week ends and those who barely work eight hours for five days and find the thought of extra work repugnant. *Technique-oriented* and *task-oriented* are terms that can be used to emphasize the fact that some organization members are concerned with procedure and others are concerned with meeting a goal no matter how. The terms *innovators* and *conservers* might describe differing attitudes toward change. Clearly, organization members may adjust in a variety of ways to their organizations, and different organizations make different demands. Consequently the word *bureaucrat* contains little behavioral information; it cannot mean much more than *organizational member*. The stereotype of the bureaucrat is a person concerned about security, obedient and rule-following, and not very forceful or imaginative. However, if the phrase *organization member* is substituted for the word *bureaucrat*, it is easy to see just how inaccurate the stereotype may be. Some members will conform to the stereotype, but not all.

A Note on Leader Behavior

It seems worthwhile, after considering patterns of adaptation to organizational life, to give some special consideration to leader behavior. Most studies of leadership divide leader behavior into two types—autocratic and democratic. Stanley Seashore calls these types *authoritarian* and *participative*.[30]

> In general, there are two basic approaches to the management of an organization—the "participative" approach based upon group decision, mutual discussion of common problems, and shared responsibility, and the "authoritarian" approach based upon strong individual leadership.

This dichotomy can be seen in some of the most significant work on leadership, the work done in the late 1940s and early 1950s by investigators at the Ohio State University. Although much of their work concerned leadership in small groups, some dealt specifically with executives and heads of formal organizations. The Ohio State researchers defined nine dimensions of leader behavior.[31] Their list was as follows:

Initiation—the frequency with which a leader originates, facilitates, or resists new ideas and new practices.

Membership—the frequency with which a leader mixes with the group, stresses informal interaction between himself and members, or interchanges personal services with members.

Representation—the frequency with which a leader defends his group against attack, advances the interests of his group, and acts in behalf of his group.

Organization—the frequency with which a leader defines or structures his own work, the work of other members, or the relationships among members in the performance of their work.

Domination—the frequency with which the leader restricts the behavior of individuals or the group in action, decision making, or expression of opinion.

Communication—the frequency with which a leader provides information to members, seeks information from them, facilitates exchange of information or shows awareness of affairs pertaining to the group.

Recognition—the frequency with which a leader engages in behavior which expresses approval or disapproval of the behavior of group members.

Production—the frequency with which a leader sets

levels of effort of achievement or prods members for greater effort achievement.

Analysis of 357 completed leader-behavior descriptions indicated that many of these dimensions were related to one another. Consequently, the nine dimensions were reduced to three.

A maintenance of membership factor—behavior that increases a leader's acceptability to the group.

Objectivity attainment—behavior high in the production and organization dimensions.

Group interaction facilitation—behavior or acts stressing the mechanics of effective interaction of group members.

More research reduced these three dimensions to two—consideration and initiating. Carroll Shartle has noted that these two dimensions, which are quite similar to the first two of the three noted above, are sometimes referred to as the *human relations* and the *get the work out* dimensions.

Closely related to the study and description of leadership is the study of the relationship between leader behavior and situation. Early in the Ohio State studies Stogdill and Shartle published an article in which they argued that leadership must be studied "as a relationship between persons, and as an aspect of organizational activities, structures, and goals."[32] Other writers, also concerned with the situation, have argued that the pattern of behavior an executive chooses should be governed by the kind of enterprise he is managing.[33] Probably most observers would agree that the situation affects the behavior of a leader, but Alex Bavelas has further suggested that the situation affects who will become a leader. In an article dealing with leadership and its situation, he wrote that "almost any member of a group may become its leader under circumstances that enable him to perform the required functions of leadership. . . ."[34] He also noted that because of differences in situation the abilities that may help a man rise to the top of an organization may prove a "positive detriment" once he reaches the top.

Although the preceding paragraphs mention only a few relevant studies, students of organization have given much attention to the division between democratic, people-oriented, participative leaders and autocratic, authoritarian, production-oriented leaders. Of course, executive behavior may not be so readily classifiable as these types suggest. Stanley Seashore has noted that consideration and initiation are independent of each other and that a person might be high on one end and either high or low on the other.[35] Certainly an executive can favor both good human relations and high production, but there is much room for variation in emphasis. Because their leaders and their tasks vary, organizations in the Executive Branch may resemble either democratic political systems or authoritarian political systems. Which they resemble may have consequences for their ability to recruit, their relations with other Executive Branch organizations, and their relations with Congress and their clienteles.

Conclusion

This chapter has presented a variety of concepts and ways of looking at formal organizations. But it may not be altogether clear how this material can help in understanding the Executive Branch. Some examples may be useful.

The social system perspective warns us constantly not to focus all our attention on what is formal—on organization charts, manuals of rules and regulations, job descriptions and classifications. Actual behavior within an organization may be quite different from what the formalities lead us to expect. Cliques or informal groups may not appear on the organization chart, but their presence may be important; if they conflict with one another the performance of the organization may be affected. Rules in a bureaucracy are important but everything the rules require is not always done. From the President on down, careful officials assume that rules are not automatically obeyed.

The authority system perspective emphasizes that within any organization many men may have or share authority, though each may have authority for different reasons and over different men and matters. Some men in positions which appear to have authority may in fact play their role as though they had little authority. Presidents and Department Secretaries, to say nothing of lesser officials, are quite capable of exercising very little of the authority of their positions. To use a sports analogy, some executives may be players, others umpires, and some may simply watch. (And there may occasionally be some who would rather not even look.) To complicate matters further, some may give consistent performances and some may play only occasionally (perhaps when they think they can win) and at other times simply watch and wait.

The authority system perspective and the political system perspective go well together. A basic question in any bureaucratic organization is, "who is going to have authority over what?" This is a political question. How much authority is the Secretary of Defense going to have vis-à-vis the Joint Chiefs of Staff? How much authority is the Secretary of State going to have vis-à-vis the U.S. Ambassador to the United Nations? These are clearly political questions. Reorganization in a government agency is likely to shift authority and responsibility, to regroup units, and reassign men—and a political struggle is likely to accompany the reorganization.

When thinking of an organization as a system of incentives, one can start by considering the resources available to the President. What incentives does he have at his disposal to get what he wants from the members of the Executive Branch? Political appointees he can hire, and sometimes fire. The President has ready access to the press, which he can use for praising or criticizing. A job well done or the expectation of such performance can lead to a visit in the President's office and a tour of the Rose Garden. The President can also pointedly ignore. Most generally the President has a large supply of incentives, but much depends on the skill with which he uses them. He cannot squander, but neither can he hoard. Many similar things could be said of other federal executives. Their stock of resources may be less varied and abundant, but the job of any executive can be understood in part as that of using the incentives he has to get the performance he desires. Moreover, what the President wants and what some other government executive wants may by no means be identical. A subordinate may then have to choose what he will do. If his immediate superior regularly observes him and controls rewards and sanctions, the prudent choice is obvious.

That organizations are status systems is most obvious in the military but plain enough in other bureaucratic organizations. Status affects office size and parking space, but more importantly it affects how much attention and respect an organization member receives. A high-ranking official, an Assistant Secretary or a Secretary or even a bureau chief in his own organization, can utter platitudes and nonsense and have them solemnly attended to. The lower one goes in the hierarchy, the harder it may be to get attention, and the more likely it is that one will be ignored. To put the point another way, whether anyone is listening depends only partially on what is being said; it depends also on who is speaking. People with high status are entitled to be listened to; that is one of the perquisites of office. An obvious danger is that nonsense will be taken for sense because it comes from someone of high status. A less obvious danger is that high-status people may overload communication channels so that lower-status organization members have no chance of being heard.

The restraints that a status system may impose on an organization's ability to innovate, to change, to reorganize, should be recognized. Men who have status are likely to want to preserve it and are likely to resist any changes that they think may lower their status. Proposals for change that do not take account of an organization's status system are likely to come to grief.

When thinking about the organization as a communication system it is useful again to focus on the President. Whom does he communicate with, through whom, and about what? On the one hand a President might communicate with everyone only through a single White House assistant, and on the other he might try to communicate personally with everyone doing something of interest to him. Clearly either extreme would be well nigh impossible, but they illustrate a Presidential problem: Any President must decide how much to rely on information that is second hand and how much to seek out for himself, directly. His time is valuable, but so is accurate information. In addition to being a receiver, a President is obviously a communicator; how clearly he communicates, how frequently, with whom, and by what means are all important questions. Of course all these questions could be asked of any other federal executive. Keep in mind also that authority is exercised through communications. If one does not communicate one cannot exercise authority. Orders, requests, suggestions, questions—all these must be communicated. And accurate information must come in.

Whether thinking about authority, or communication, or incentives, or other aspects of organizations, remember that individuals adjust to their work and organizational life in a variety of ways. Some will seek power enthusiastically and others will shrink from its exercise. Some will have a passion for anonymity, and others crave publicity as strongly. Some may devote themselves to their work, and some may use their salaries to devote themselves to other things. Some may be loyal to their organization, some to their profession, and some only to themselves. The organizations in the Executive Branch may be composed of unknown bureaucrats, but they are surely composed of individuals, as well.

Notes for Chapter 4

1. The literature on formal organizations is vast. Among the most useful surveys are: James G. March and Herbert Simon, *Organizations* (New York: John Wiley and Sons, 1958);

Peter M. Blau and W. Richard Scott, *Formal Organizations* (San Francisco: Chandler Publishing Co., 1962); Theodore Caplow, *Principles of Organization* (New York: Harcourt, Brace and World, Inc. 1964); James G. March (ed.), *Handbook of Organizations* (Chicago: Rand McNally and Co., 1965); Daniel Katz and Robert L. Kahn, *The Social Psychology of Organizations* (New York: John Wiley and Sons, Inc., 1966); Anthony Downs, *Inside Bureaucracy* (Boston: Little, Brown and Co., 1967). All of these books contain extensive bibliographies.

2. T. Caplow, *op. cit.*, p. 1.

3. D. M. Blau and W. R. Scott, *op. cit.*, p. 1.

4. Edgar H. Schein, *Organizational Psychology* (Englewood Cliffs, N.J., Prentice-Hall, Inc., 1965), p. 8.

5. Richard H. Hall, "The Concept of Bureaucracy: An Empirical Assessment," *American Journal of Sociology,* vol. 69 (1963), pp. 32–40. See especially p. 34.

6. This perspective is discussed in less detail than the others in the sections below. For an insightful study see Erving Goffman, *The Presentation of Self in Everyday Life* (Garden City, N.Y.: Doubleday Anchor Books, 1959).

7. T. Caplow, *op sit.*, p. 1.

8. Herbert Kaufman, *The Forest Ranger* (Baltimore: Johns Hopkins Press, 1960), p. 102.

9. For a particularly relevant discussion of this perspective see Herbert Kaufman, "Organization Theory and Political Theory," *American Political Science Review,* LVII (1964), pp. 5–14.

10. Chester I. Barnard, *The Functions of the Executive* (Cambridge: Harvard University Press, 1938). See Chapter IX, "The Economy of Incentives."

11. Peter B. Clark and James Q. Wilson, "Incentive Systems: A Theory of Organizations," *Administrative Science Quarterly,* vol. 6 (1961), pp. 129–166.

12. Richard E. Neustadt, *Presidential Power* (New York: John Wiley and Sons, Inc., 1961), pp. 19–27.

13. William H. Whyte, *The Organization Man* (New York: Simon and Schuster, 1956), p. 3.

14. Robert Presthus, *The Organizational Society* (New York: Alfred A. Knopf, 1962), p. 167.

15. *Ibid.*, p. 208.

16. *Ibid.*, p. 208.

17. *Ibid.,* p. 281.

18. *Ibid.,* p. 258.

19. *Ibid.,* p. 179.

20. Alvin W. Gouldner, "Cosmopolitans and Locals: Toward An Analysis of Latent Social Roles," *Administrative Science Quarterly,* 2 (1957–58), pp. 281–306 and 444–480.

21. R. Presthus, *op cit.,* p. 259.

22. Leonard Reissman, "A Study of Role Conceptions in Bureaucracy," *Social Forces,* 27 (1949), pp. 305–310.

23. Dwaine Marvick, *Career Perspectives in a Bureaucratic Setting* (Ann Arbor: Univeristy of Michigan Press, 1954).

24. Jonathan A. Slesinger, *Personnel Adaptations in the Federal Junior Management Assistant Program* ('Ann Arbor: Institute of Public Administration, University of Michigan, 1961).

25. Ralph H. Turner, "The Navy Disbursing Officer as a Bureaucrat," *American Sociological Review,* 12 (1947), pp. 342–348.

26. *Ibid.,* p. 347.

27. *Ibid.,* p. 347.

28. Robert K. Merton, "Bureaucratic Structure and Personality," in his *Social Theory and Social Structure* (Glencoe: The Free Press, 1957), pp. 195–206.

29. See the extensive discussion of various patterns of adaptation in Bertram M. Gross, *The Managing of Organizations* (New York: The Free Press, 1964), vol. 1, chapter 16.

30. Stanley E. Seashore, "Administrative Leadership and Organizational Effectiveness," in Rensis Likert and Samuel P. Hayes, Jr., (eds.), *Some Applications of Behavioral Research* (Paris: UNESCO, 1957), p. 47.

31. Carroll L. Shartle, *Executive Performance and Leadership* (Englewood Cliffs, N.J.: Prentice-Hall, Inc., 1956), pp. 116–123. See also John K. Hemphill and Alvin E. Coons, "Development of the Leader Behavior Description Questionnaire," in Ralph M. Stogdill and A. C. Coons, *Leader Behavior: Its Description and Measurement* (Columbus: Bureau of Business Research, College of Commerce and Administration, Ohio State University, 1957, pp. 6–38.

32. See Ralph M. Stogdill and Carroll L. Shartle, *Patterns of Administrative Performance* (Columbus: Bureau of Business Research, College of Commerce and Administration, Ohio State University, 1956), p. 286.

33. See for example Robert Tannenbaum and W. H.

Schmidt, "How to Choose a Leadership Pattern," *Harvard Business Review,* 36 (March–April 1958), pp. 95–101; and also Robert T. Golembiewski, "Three Styles of Leadership and Their Uses," *Personnel,* 38 (July–August 1961), pp. 34–43.

34. Alex Bavelas, "Leadership: Man and Function," *Administrative Science Quarterly,* 4 (1960), p. 494.

35. S. E. Seashore, *op. cit.,* p. 16.

THE EXECUTIVE
BRANCH IN THE
POLITICAL SYSTEM

Now that we have learned something about the organizations and personnel of the Executive Branch, we can go on to consider in more detail their relations with the President, the Congress, and other participants in American politics. This chapter attempts to provide an overview. Following chapters deal with program development, budget-making, and reorganizations; all these activities bring the Executive Branch into contact with other parts of the American political system.

The Political System

No doubt most of those reading this book know a fair amount about American politics, and a lengthy in-

Notes for this chapter appear on pages 147–148.

troductory description would be out of place. Nor need
an elaborate definition of the term *political system* de-
tain us. Brief comment on this term may be useful,
however; and we should be clear about the components
and characteristics of the American political system
that the discussion here assumes.

The term *political system* is currently fashionable
in political science, and it may be made quite complex.[1]
Here, however, the term political system simply refers to
the many different institutions, organizations, and individual decision-makers in American politics and their
interaction with one another. The political system includes the Congress, the President, the Court, and the
bureaucracy; it also includes organized interest groups,
political parties, and individuals as voters and expressors
of opinion.

It is obvious from this list of participants that one
characteristic of the American political system is pluralism. This characteristic is critical, because it means that
many participants may demand a voice in governmental
decision-making. The pluralism of American politics
means that any bureau chief may have to serve several
masters. One cannot understand bureaucratic behavior
unless one appreciates this fact of bureaucratic life. The
pluralism of American politics has other implications.
Many participants compete for power, for influence. This
competition exists on various levels and for a variety of
reasons. Congress and the President may compete for
power over the bureaucracy; each may want to have the
last say. The Bureau of the Budget and the House Appropriations Committee may not compete in so many
words, but certainly each hopes that it can make its
decisions stick. There is also competition among the
executives and organizations of the Executive Branch—
competition for programs, for money, for prestige.

Not only do we have a pluralistic politics, we also have a coalition politics, perhaps just because there are so many participants. On any particular issue or in any particular conflict there is likely to be an attempt by the affected parties to gather allies. Is the Department of Agriculture quarreling with the General Services Administration over the use of the GSA motor pools? Each may try to enlist the support of the Budget Bureau and ultimately the President. Is a Congressional committee about to investigate the Office of Economic Opportunity? Numerous social welfare organizations may be called on to attest to the value of the OEO. Has the President ordered a cut in the Air Force budget? Perhaps appropriations committee members can be persuaded to put back the money. Coalition building goes on not only in the offices and cloakrooms of Congress as votes are being sought or off the convention floor as time for nomination approaches, but also as Executive Branch agencies try to build and protect their budgets, programs, and organizations.

The American political system exhibits two other characteristics: it is bipolar and fluid. Perhaps another way of saying that American politics is bipolar is to say that we have a politics of pro and con. Politics in this country seems often (not always of course) to be a two-sided game. Even though we have a pluralistic politics, in a particular conflict there are likely to be just two sides, and coalitions build up on one side or the other. The coalitions are not necessarily the same from issue to issue, which is what is meant by the statement that we have a fluid politics. To be sure there are a few relatively stable alliances; for example, organized labor and civil rights groups. But many coalitions are ad hoc; they are oriented around a particular bill or issue, and when their *raison d'être* passes so may they.

As one tries to describe the American political system, other words come to mind—nonideological, pragmatic, bargaining, compromising. Perhaps all these are suggested or implied by the notion of coalition politics, but it is well to make them explicit. They can be applied not only to the American political system as a whole but also to the Executive Branch agencies in particular. Each agency wants to survive and if possible to prosper, and to achieve these goals the leaders will bargain and make compromises, guided less by doctrine than by the existing situation and their goal of organizational well-being.

The Executive Branch and the President

The first chapter emphasized that the Executive Branch is much more than the President, and must be distinguished from the President. It is possible to view the President and the Executive Branch as separate branches, with one or the other being the fourth branch of government; or it is possible to view them both as components of one unit, much as the House and Senate are different components of the Congress. But the important point is that the President and the Executive Branch are not the same. The distinction has been stressed by Arthur Schlesinger, Jr. in his book on the presidency of John F. Kennedy.[2]

> Kennedy was fully sensitive—perhaps oversensitive—to the limitations imposed by Congress on the presidential freedom of manoeuver. But, though he was well aware of the problem within the executive domain, I do not think he had entirely appreciated its magnitude. The textbooks had talked of three coordinate branches of government: the executive, the

legislative, the judiciary. But with an activist president it became apparent that there was a fourth branch: the Presidency itself. And, in pursuing his purposes, the President was likely to encounter almost as much resistance from the executive branch as from the others. By 1961 the tension between the permanent government and the presidential government was deep in our system.[2]

But to speak of a gulf between the presidential government and the permanent government may be misleading; it may suggest that the Executive Branch or permanent government is united and cohesive, though separated from the President. Yet this is not so. Indeed, the Executive Branch is so far from being cohesive that one cannot speak meaningfully of the President's relationship with it. Rather one must think of the President's relationship with particular organizations within the Executive Branch—his relations, for example, with the State Department, the Defense Department, the FBI, the Corps of Engineers, the Civil Service Commission, and so on. To complicate matters further, one must remember the importance of personalities and circumstances. Different Presidents may have different relationships with the same organizations, and the same President may not have the same relationship with two Secretaries of State or Treasury. It is relevant to recall a point made earlier: two men who occupy the same position may play the role differently.

The Constitution makes clear that the President is the superior officer of the Executive Branch. In addition to a general statement vesting the executive power in the President of the United States, the Constitution confers particular powers and responsibilities on the President. He is Commander-in-Chief; he has substantial power of appointment; he makes treaties; he requires from department heads their opinions about matters within their jurisdiction; he must submit to Congress periodically a state of the union message; he recommends to Congress measures that he thinks appropriate; and he "shall take care that the laws be faithfully executed." The Constitution, in short, establishes a superior-subordinate relationship between the President and the Executive Branch. Both tradition and particular statutes enforce this view. The authority given by the Congress to the President for preparing an annual budget is one example, and the authority granted to the President by Congress to reorganize organizations within the Executive Branch is another. But despite the Constitution, tradition, the law, and folklore, the President is frequently not chief of the Executive Branch. He is more accurately viewed as chief persuader and chief bargainer.[3]

If the President is viewed as only one of several players in the game of politics, it is easy to understand that he is not and cannot be the ruler of the Executive Branch. We realize that the President may have to rely on persuasion or patronage to get what he wants from Congressmen; that these are also required when it comes to ostensible subordinates in the Executive Branch contradicts our myths. Nevertheless there is no more accurate way to view the Executive Branch than as a political arena. The President may be more than "first among equals," but he is hardly the only man with power. The support that other officials may draw from Congressional committee chairmen or from influential groups or from public opinion can give them a base of independent power, a base protected from the effects of Presidential displeasure. Not every official can be independent, of course. Not every official enjoys the cordial relationship with Capitol Hill that J. Edgar Hoover has had. Some officials need the President and thus are subject to his influence. But those who do not need the President may be hard to influence.

If the President is considered only one participant in the political arena, if it is understood that he will not get his way simply because he is President, then we can ask: How can the President get what he is after? How can he motivate people to do what he wants them to do? How can he influence the behavior of other participants? The answer of course is, "through the skillful use of incentives and sanctions, rewards and punishments." The word skillful should be emphasized because, as we have noted earlier, not all subordinates will respond in the same way to the same incentive or sanction. Men have different needs, different values, different preferences, and indeed different friends. Yet in practice we often assume that the same reward will entice all men. A President with insight knows better and becomes aware of what will move particular subordinates so that he can use the resources of his office to best advantage.

What are the resources of his office? What rewards does he have to dispense, and what punishments? To begin with, the President has some power to hire and fire. But this power, as we have seen, is limited in several ways. The vast majority of Executive Branch personnel are career personnel who are neither hired nor fired by the President; and in selecting the men he can appoint, the President operates under numerous constraints. He cannot by any means always hire the man he wants, nor can be replace whoever displeases him.

How can the President reward the men who work for him? The President can show interest in an Executive Branch organization, a program, or a person, and in so doing encourage action that he wants. He can praise and give publicity. He can allow an organization to increase in size and permit substantial increases when the annual budget is prepared. To orders meant to control growth or to budget cutbacks he can grant exceptions. In inter-agency disputes he can support one agency or another. What sanctions does the President have? He can ignore instead of notice and be bored instead of interested. He can withhold funds and change the allocation of respon-sibilities. He can reorganize an agency out of existence, and he can publicly fix responsibility.

In distributing rewards and sanctions the Presi-dent operates within flexible but real limits. The use of rewards and sanctions has its costs—monetary, political, administrative—and in some circumstances action may be just too costly. Because he may not be able to afford to act, a President may be unable to influence nominal subordinates and indeed may have to tolerate their ig-noring him. Even when he does act, his action may be ineffective. A President may cut an agency budget in retribution, but the money may be restored with interest by the Congress—particularly if the opposition party is in control. By the same token, the money that a Presi-dent gives as reward may be stripped away by a hostile Congress. The reorganization that the President suggests may be vetoed by the Congress.

There are other limits. Even if he wished to the President might not be able to give monetary rewards to all he thought deserving simply because there is not likely to be enough money available. The President can give attention and praise, but Presidential praise may not warm the hearts of all officials and praising one man may incur another's wrath. In decisions involving inter-agency disputes the President must be aware of the precedent his decision will set and its possible effect on a variety of Presidential goals. The sum of these obser-vations is that at any particular time there will be some officials and some organizations not subject to the Presi-dent's influence.

The Executive Branch and the Congress

Congress is no more a monolithic body than the Executive Branch. It is first two separate houses; second, it is a collection of committees; and third, it is 535 individuals. Congress is composed of two houses—both with substantial power. The obvious implication is that any government executive should not only cultivate friendship in at least one house, he should avoid hostility from either. Committees in both houses have a hand in the fiscal and structural well-being of government organizations, and the anger of either house can be unsettling. The existence of two houses can on occasion be beneficial as far as an executive is concerned (a Senate committee may put back what a House committee takes away), but there is little question that the resulting duplication in committees complicates an executive's life.

One of the most crucial characteristics of Congress is that it is composed of committees; in fact, it is not far from the truth to say that Congress *is* its committees. The business of the government is too vast to permit the Congress as a whole to oversee it; in practice the powers of Congress are exercised by standing committees organized along subject-matter lines.

SENATE COMMITTEES	HOUSE COMMITTEES
Aeronautical and Space Sciences	Agriculture
Agriculture and forestry	Appropriations
Appropriations	Armed Services
Armed Services	Banking and Currency
Banking and Currency	District of Columbia
Commerce	Education and Labor
District of Columbia	Foreign Affairs
	Government Operations

Finance
Foreign Relations
Government Operations
Interior and Insular
　Affairs
Judiciary
Labor and Public
　Welfare
Post Office and Civil
　Service
Public Works
Rules and
　Administration

House Administration
Interior and Insular
　Affairs
Interstate and Foreign
　Commerce
Judiciary
Merchant Marine and
　Fisheries
Post Office and Civil
　Service
Public Works
Rules
Science and Astronautics
Un-American Activities
Veterans Affairs
Ways and Means

What are the powers of Congress that these committees exercise? Congress appropriates money for the conduct of the government; every January the President sends a budget message to Congress, and in due course Congress responds. Congressional action however, reflects decisions made in the subcommittees of the House and Senate Appropriations committees. Thus Congressional appropriations subcommittees have jurisdiction over the financing of executive organizations. Other standing committees consider proposed legislation affecting the organizations and must authorize all requests for funds. Presidential messages on everything from poverty and civil rights to taxation and agriculture are considered by one committee or another, as are direct agency requests for legislation. Not only substantive matters but also organizational problems concern the committees. Reorganization proposals of the President can be vetoed by either house, in effect, by a committee of either house. Both House and Senate committees can hold hearings and carry out investigations which may result in legislation or in executive reorganization. And of course Senate committees review the qualifications of men being appointed to public office by the President.

One of the topics in virtually all public administration texts is "Congressional Control of Administration."[4] In practice this becomes committee examination and control of particular organizations. Government executives must be particularly concerned with the views, actions, and reactions of four Congressional committees —two in the House and two in the Senate. In the House of Representatives the views of the appropriations committee and especially its relevant subcommittee must be attended to, as must the views of the committee in charge of the field of an organization's legislation. In the Senate the corresponding organizations are important— the Senate appropriations committee and the relevant substantive committee. To these four committees must on occasion be added the House and Senate committees on government operations, which have a very broad grant of authority and can inquire into virtually anything. The Senate Government Operations Committee in particular has provided a base for many an investigation into this or that organization in the Executive Branch.

It is even more precise to say that the government executive is most likely to be concerned to maintain contact with, to please, to mollify, or to persuade the four men who head the four important committees. Bureaucrats know as well as political scientists that many a chairman is the committee. With the chairman on his side an administrator may have the committee; with the chairman against him the rest may make little difference. No executive would if he could help it offend the ranking minority member of a committee (he might be the chairman after the next election) nor indeed any of the committee members, but first and foremost come the interests of the chairman. The views of the committee's chief clerk (head of the committee staff) are also important, as they are likely to reflect (and also influence) the views of the chairman. Budget officers and other bureaucrats ignore chief clerks at their peril.

All government executives are by no means equally concerned with Congress and its committees. Relations with Congress are so important that top executives (Secretaries and their immediate assistants, agency heads, bureau chiefs) devote a substantial amount of time to communicating with and trying to persuade Congressmen. Department Secretaries regularly and repeatedly testify before House and Senate committees. In addition many departments have assistant secretaries whose main or sole task is liaison with Congress. Below the departmental level specific positions for legislative liaison are less common; but bureau chiefs testify before committees, and their budget officers are frequently in contact with appropriations committee staff.

Given the importance of Congress and its committees, it is small wonder that executive agencies are attentive and courteous to Congressmen, devote resources to the care of Congressmen, and allocate resources and make decisions that will benefit influential Congressmen. Inquiries and letters from Congressmen are answered promptly, often under a 24-hour rule that requires Congressional correspondence to be at least acknowledged if not fully answered within 24 hours of receipt. Research may be done for Congressmen and speeches written. Bureaus and departments are more than willing to help a Congressman draft legislation that pertains to them. If a Congressman wants to go out into the field to inspect a facility, the concerned organization will gladly arrange the trip and may provide the transportation. Favorable decisions affecting a particular district or state (announcement of a large government contract or a new post office) may be announced through a Congressman's or Senator's office. And of course facilities may be put in states or districts where they may do some legislative good. It is not entirely accidental that some southern states have a considerable number of military installations. Until a few years ago the chairman of the Senate Armed Services Committee came from Georgia, and so did the chairman of the House Armed Services Committee. Now the chairman of the Senate Armed Services Committee comes from Mississippi and the chairman of the House Armed Services Committee comes from North Carolina.

Not all executive organizations are in an equally good position for doing favors and building support in Congress. At one extreme are the Armed Forces, which can arrange inspection tours to European bases or the naval base at Honolulu. In addition they maintain facilities in numerous states and are constantly awarding sizable contracts. They can assign many men to Congressional liaison and still accomplish their mission without strain. Smaller organizations may not be able to devote such substantial resources to the cause of Congressional good will, and of course many organizations carry out programs that do not lend themselves to gaining Congressional support.

For all the formal power of Congress, Congress does operate under important restraints in playing its role of administrative overseer. Congress is relatively small compared to the Executive Branch; it does not meet continuously, it is made up (at best) of intelligent laymen, and it has limited staff. These characteristics mean that Congress is unable to review the performance of Executive Branch organizations in any regular and systematic way. Because of its limited staff Congress cannot collect all the information it would need to review agency performance systematically and, if it could collect the needed information, it could not analyze and interpret it. Congress can at most spot-check what is going on in the Executive Branch. It can react to complaints, respond to fires. But it may be able to spot fires only when they have reached considerable proportions. Samuel Huntington has suggested that initiative in policy has passed from the Congress to the Executive Branch, and with this observation there can be little quarrel. But he has also suggested that the pre-eminent role of Congress today is oversight of administration.[5] This suggestion seems open to question, especially if oversight means regular systematic checking rather than intermittent looks.

An additional limit on Congress's ability to oversee administration is the potential ability of a government executive to avoid the close examination of his organization and its budget by maintaining friendly personal relations with relevant committee chairmen. If a bureau chief can build an atmosphere of confidence and trust, then Congressmen may not ask him many questions and may accept on faith his answers to any questions asked. To the Congressman this process is perfectly rational; with a limited amount of time he chooses to focus most closely on those organizations that he does not know or trust. It makes sense, therefore, for a bureau chief to try to win over a committee chairman, but such personal relations may interfere with proper Congressional oversight of administration.

Today the work of the central control agencies in the Executive Branch, in particular the White House Office, the Bureau of the Budget, the Civil Service Commission, and the General Services Administration may to some extent fill the gaps in Congressional oversight. Today it may be that not only policy initiation but also oversight of administration has moved to the Executive Branch. Still, Congress can hardly be ignored. Because the actions and interests of Congressmen are not always predictable, because the public's interest in issues is not constant, and because a familiar Congressman may lose an election and be replaced by a stranger, government executives must always be watching Congress. The actions of a Congressman and his committee can still wreak havoc on a program and an organization. Government executives know this and act accordingly.

The Executive Branch and the Judiciary

What is the relationship between Executive Branch organizations and the federal courts? Do the courts act as a check on actions of administrative agencies? They may, or they may not. The first and most important point to remember is that most administrative activity is *not* reviewed in the courts. Martin Shapiro makes this point in *The Supreme Court and Administrative Agencies.*[6]

> . . . courts provide almost no effective check on what we typically think of as administration. When the Corps of Engineers builds a dam or when the Department of Health, Education, and Welfare prepares a research study on overcrowding in urban schools, there is almost no opportunity for judicial check on how efficiently, accurately, or fairly these agencies

conduct their actual operations. The planning, research and development, spending and physical operation—hauling mail, printing money, storing grain—of administrative agencies are largely beyond the realm of judicial inspection. Indeed most of the business of administrative agencies is conducted in the same way as the business of large corporations—by correspondence, consultations, interoffice memos, and telephone calls, all of which rarely rise to legal significance. A very large share of even those agency decisions that do directly affect the legal rights of individual citizens cannot be appealed to the courts and an even larger share are not so appealed. Thus courts do not provide much of a check on the general operations of administrative agencies, the millions of decisions, actions, and physical operations that turn words on the statute books into tuberculosis vaccines, hot meals for school children, rockets, national parks, and college dormitories.

Some administrative activity can be and often is reviewed in the courts. "Roughly 20 per cent of the Supreme Court's written opinions concern administrative decisions."[7] Much of the legislation that Congress passes is very general and is implemented by rules and regulations developed by Executive Branch agencies. The courts may be asked to determine whether these elaborations are consistent with the parent statute and whether they have been properly applied, as well as whether the parent statute, the implementing rules, and the actions of the administrative agencies conform to the requirements of the Constitution.

How can the courts go about this task? They may examine the performance of administrative agencies when an agency asks that its rules and orders be enforced. If the Selective Service System takes a man to court for failing to report for induction, the court may study the work of the Selective Service System and determine that the man being prosecuted was improperly classified. (Of course the Selective Service System will try not to go to court unless it is fairly sure that its action accords with the law and is thus likely to be upheld. Weak cases can lead to bad precedents.) If the Internal Revenue Service takes a man to court for failing to pay his taxes, the court may have an opportunity to find out how the agency collected its evidence and whether its rules are consistent with the intent of Congress. Of course, citizens do not always have to be prosecuted in the courts before they can challenge an administrative agency; in some circumstances they can initiate a challenge to administrative agencies.

Shapiro stresses, however, "that the overwhelmingly typical action of courts exercising review is to refuse to substitute their own decisions for those of the agency, and that only in a handful of the thousands of agency decisions made each year is there even an effort by the adversely effected party to get a second decision from the courts."[8]

In the field of administrative law, much attention is given to the particular circumstances in which appeals from administrative decisions may be taken to court and the grounds on which courts may overrule administrative decisions, but these topics can be passed over here. It suffices to say that there are many areas into which courts will not go, and the citizen is left with the results of administrative activity.

The Executive Branch and Interest Groups

If one looks even cursorily at the American society and economy he finds a number of lines of cleavage—

labor, business, agriculture, cities, Negroes. These sectors of the society and the economy represent major interests, they have particular wants and needs, and they make demands, sometimes conflicting demands, on the government. These groups are far from homogeneous (small business and the giant corporation, the family farmer and the corporate farmer), and each contains a number of formally organized associations. It is these formally organized associations—the AFL–CIO, the United States Chamber of Commerce, the American Farm Bureau Federation, the Farmer's Union, the NAACP, the Southern Christian Leadership Conference —that can usefully be thought of as interest groups. In addition, many professional or occupational interests are organized formally; the American Medical Association and the American Bar Association are examples. The National Rifle Association (NRA) is an organized interest group based on a widely shared hobby. A glance at the long list of clubs and organizations included annually in the *World Almanac* will provide many more examples.

Though interest groups have quite different views and aims they do have many common characteristics. Although they may formally provide for membership participation in the selection of officers and in the taking of positions, many large organizations are run by relatively small groups of very active members aided by professional staffs. Many members may be relatively passive and apathetic, content to pay their dues and leave the running of the organization to others. Another characteristic of interest groups is that, unlike political parties, they are out to gain not office but particular policies. They may, of course, try to get men in office as a means to this end. Because they are interested in public policy, many of the major organized groups have headquarters in Washington, where they are in position to work for the legislative and administrative action that they want. In addition to these major groups, many *ad hoc* groups may be in Washington at any time pressing particular causes and fighting for or against particular bills in Congress. After a Congressional session or two, they have gotten what they wanted or have been soundly defeated, they may disappear while their places are taken by new associations of the moment.

Both the many continuing groups and the short-lived groups use lobbyists. Just as a major organization may have a lawyer, so it may have a lobbyist—though that probably will not be his title. The lobbyist is responsible for day-to-day contact with officialdom and for keeping track of government action and inaction. He may not testify on pending legislation or rules—leaving that to officers of the group he works for—but he may certainly help prepare their testimony, he may try to see that they are asked the right questions, and he may even be instrumental in arranging the hearings in the first place. Substantial groups (organized labor, the NRA) may have lobbyists on their full-time staff, but smaller organizations and *ad hoc* groups are more likely to retain lobbyists (or public relations counsel) for a limited period. At any one time a public relations firm in Washington may have several interest groups as clients.

Interest groups may try to obtain what they want from the government in several ways. They may take part in political campaigns by endorsing candidates, by contributing funds to a campaign, and by trying to get their members to vote for particular men, in the hope that friendly men in Congress will benefit the group. Interest groups may take a more or less direct part in the legislative process. Interest group representatives may testify on pending bills that affect them, and they may approach particular Representatives and Senators to argue the merits of particular bills. Much of this activity is simply informative, but information is vital and may be appreciated. Interest groups may promise or imply support in coming elections in return for appropriate votes on the floor of Congress, and they may threaten opposition if a Congressman votes otherwise. In addition to the campaign and Capitol Hill activity, interest groups may try to influence public opinion and thus affect Congressmen indirectly. Interest groups may also go to court to get what they want, particularly if they think they cannot get it from the Congress or administrative bodies.

What is the role of interest groups in the bureaucracy? Executive Branch organizations initiate much legislation, and interest groups have a chance to get in on the ground floor when a bill is being drafted if they can exercise influence within a federal agency. Interest groups concerned with the education programs of the federal government know that they are likely to take shape in the Office of Education in the Department of Health, Education and Welfare. Federal programs affecting urban areas may begin in the Department of Housing and Urban Affairs. If an interest group does not have access to these agencies it may not be able to affect legislation in its early stages.

After a bill has been passed it must be implemented, and interest groups again focus their attention on what happens in administrative agencies. Laws may be enforced vigorously or halfheartedly, and the difference may be important. Legislation passed by Congress may be general, giving an administrative agency power to write detailed regulations. The automobile safety legislation passed by Congress delegates authority to the National Traffic Safety Bureau to prepare detailed safety standards for automobiles. Naturally the automobile industry is interested in the content of these standards, so it pays close attention to the work of the Bureau and expresses its views formally and informally, publicly and privately, in the hope that the economic impact of the safety standards on it can be lessened. In the same way agricultural groups are interested in the activity of the Department of Agriculture, lumber companies are interested in the work of the Forest Service, and conservation groups are interested in decisions of the Secretary of Interior.

To enhance the chances of being influential within the government, interest groups often try to get their own organizations in the Executive Branch. A glance at the organizational structure of the Executive Branch gives a fairly accurate though somewhat dated notion of the influential interests in the country. Major social and economic sectors have cabinet departments. Special groups of some importance may be represented by independent agencies or have their own offices and bureaus. Why do interest groups want their own organization? Because with their own organization they know where to go when they want something, and they do not have to compete for attention. Administration of a program may be easier to affect if it is administered by a more or less single-purpose organization. Doubtless it is easier for the American Legion to influence the Veterans' Administration than it would be the Department of Health, Education and Welfare—so there is a Veterans' Administration carrying out programs very similar to the programs of HEW. From an interest group's point of view, their own organization may be easier to co-opt. (Of course, for this reason the creation of a specialized organization may be resisted by others not identified with that particular interest group.)

If an interest group does not have its own organization, creating one may be one of its goals; a reorganization may be proposed that would create an organization to give special attention to the interests of the concerned group. It is common for groups to propose giving their organizations cabinet rank or to suggest that their concerns deserve the attention of an organization located within the Executive Office of the President.

From an interest group's point of view it is not enough for an organization working on the interest group's problems to exist; it is also important that the interest group be influential within that organization. To this end, interest groups may try to exercise some control over staff appointments in agencies relevant to them. Of course they can exercise little or no control over civil service positions, but they may be able to influence the selection of political appointees. If they cannot actually recommend who should get a job, they may at least be able to exercise a veto. Their goal, of course, is an administrator and top staff who are sympathetic and responsive. However, interest groups may compete for influence; consumers groups and industry groups may both want to influence regulatory organizations. And it is not unhead of for one group to get the organization it wanted, only to find it staffed with representatives of opposed groups. Such are the results of political compromise.

An interest group may ask an agency to appoint advisory committees made up of representatives of those affected by the agency's programs. Conversely, organizations that desire independence may resist appointing advisory committees in order to avoid being controlled by affected groups. Public hearings on proposed regulations allow interest groups to affect the administrative process, and agencies are often required by legislation to conduct public hearings before implementing new regulations. Agencies may also be required to provide an opportunity for citizens and groups to file written comments on proposed regulations.

If interest groups are unsuccessful in gaining access to administrative agencies or if they have not been influential, they may try to move an agency indirectly through Congress or the courts. If an interest group can enlist on its side an influential Congressman or a committee with jurisdiction over its agency, then it may get what it wants. A simple opinion or wish on the part of a Congressman may be all that is needed to move an administrative agency in the desired direction; if not, there is always the threat of legislation. If a group does not have access to Congress, there remains the possibility of litigation, based on the possibility that the courts may require an administrative agency to act in a certain desired way.

So far the discussion has focused mainly on groups trying to sway administrative agencies, but the other side of the agency-interest group relationship is also important. Interest groups can provide support for administrative agencies, help them gain desirable ends, and resist undesirable ones. Conservation groups will ally willingly with the National Park Service in an attempt to set aside more land for outdoor recreation use. Educational groups will assist the Office of Education, and social welfare groups have aligned themselves with the Office of Economic Opportunity. Government agencies without associated interest groups may be tempted to create their own. Without strong interest-group support, the autonomy of an agency within the

Executive Branch is reduced; with strong interest-group support, an agency is in a better position to attempt to resist the President or the Congress.

Interest groups want certain kinds of programs and actions; government agencies may want the same or similar programs. Interest groups and government agencies are likely to have much in common and often coalesce. It is not entirely accurate to view administrative organizations simply as official interest groups—the counterparts of interest groups in the unofficial political arena—but there is some truth in the idea. Certainly interest groups and administrative organizations are often members of the same coalition working toward the same goals.

The Executive Branch and Public Opinion

The agencies of the Executive Branch operate more or less in the open, subject to public view. What they do is affected by public opinion. In the words of V. O. Key, Jr.:[10]

> Government may be regarded as operating within a context of public opinion that conditions its actions. The context is not a rigid matrix that fixes a precise form for government action. Nor is it unchangeable. It consists of opinions irregularly distributed among the people and of varying intensity, of attitudes of differing convertibility into votes, and of sentiments not always readily capable of appraisal. Yet that context, as it is perceived by those responsible for action, conditions many of the acts of those who must make what we may call "opinion related decisions." The opinion context may affect the substance of action, the form of action, or the manner of action.

These sentences indicate just how complex and indirect the link between public opinion and agency action may be.

Key's phrase, "opinions irregularly distributed among the people," is particularly important; most of the population knows very little about Executive Branch agencies. There is thus no meaningful context of public opinion for much Executive Branch action. But particular segments of the population, interested in the work of a particular agency, may have both information and opinions which affect agency action.

Agencies operate not only within an opinion context but also within a context of status and influence. The opinions of the men representing organized and substantial groups may carry more weight than the opinions of numerous unorganized individuals—if the opinions of the latter are even known. The opinions of a few Congressmen and a committee chairman are likely to be weighty indeed. In the end, whose opinions are heeded may be a matter of whose support is needed.

Government agencies may be affected by outside opinion; they may in turn try to alter it by building a favorable impression of themselves and their programs.[11] It is in an agency's interest to be viewed as working in the public interest (whatever that may mean) and carrying out its programs efficiently, economically, and effectively. And it is certainly in its interest not to have the reverse image. In testimony before Congress, in public speeches, in reports and news releases, officials of agencies try to emphasize the good their agency is doing and to explain or ignore alleged or real deficiencies. Many agencies have public information personnel to provide information and to cooperate with writers and broadcasters. Law-enforcement agencies and the military services have been particularly famous for their image-building activities on television and movie screens. The opposite side of the publicity coin is secrecy, or *official use*. Much secrecy can be justified on grounds of military necessity and national security, and more can be explained on grounds of individual privacy, but doubtless some can be understood as simply a result of protective organizational image-building.

Conclusion

It is important to remember the pluralism, the heterogeneity, of the Executive Branch. This branch reflects the pluralism of the U.S. political system, and the President may have as much trouble getting what he wants from the bureaucracy as from Congress. Between the President and some executive organizations there may be a community of interest which will result in cooperation. However, other organizations may prefer independence to cooperation with the President, and if they have other allies and sources of support they may not need him. The existence of the Congress and strong interest groups means that the executive bureaucracy is only partially under the control of the Chief Executive. The Chief Executive and the organizations of the Executive Branch have very different points of view. The organizations are specialized, parochial, self-interested. Each presses, however skillfully or successfully, for its own interests. The President, on the other hand, has a government-wide point of view to some extent and certainly has government-wide responsibilities. This difference in point of view may explain the frequent antagonism between the President and Executive Branch organizations—and the frequent alliances among the organizations, specialized Congressional committees, and interest groups.

So much attention is given the politics of bureaucracy because this is a frequently less visible and less familiar aspect of American politics. Yet the outcomes of the conflicts in, over, and between Executive Branch organizations have much to do with the substance of American public policy. No one can hope to understand how policy is formulated without some appreciation and awareness of Executive Branch politics.

Notes for Chapter 5

1. See David Easton, *A Systems Analysis of Political Life* (New York: John Wiley and Sons, Inc. 1965) and also his *A Framework For Political Analysis* (Englewood Cliffs, N.J.: Prentice-Hall, Inc., 1965).

2. Arthur M. Schlesinger, Jr., *A Thousand Days* (Boston: Houghton Mifflin Co., 1965), p. 680.

3. This is nowhere made clearer than in Richard Neustadt's book, *Presidential Power*.

4. See also Joseph P. Harris, *Congressional Control of Administration* (Washington: The Brookings Institution, 1964).

5. S. P. Huntington, *op. cit.*, p. 24.

6. Martin Shapiro, *The Supreme Court and Administrative Agencies* (New York: The Free Press, 1968), p. 13.

7. *Ibid.*, p. 13.

8. *Ibid.*, p. 95.

9. David B. Truman, *The Governmental Process* (New York: Alfred A. Knopf, 1951).

10. V. O. Key, Jr., *Public Opinion and American Democracy* (New York: Alfred A. Knopf, 1964), p. 423.

11. See Francis E. Rourke, *Secrecy and Publicity* (Baltimore: The Johns Hopkins Press, 1961).

CHANGE,
PROBLEM-SOLVING,
AND PROGRAM
DEVELOPMENT

Over the last fifty years the Executive Branch has changed dramatically. It contains more organizations, more programs, more personnel than ever before, and of course the budget is bigger. These changes can be viewed as responses to the demands of private citizens, groups, and officials and also as responses to changes in the environment. There is little question that the Executive Branch organizations have responded to changes in the society and the economy, although whether they have responded adequately may be a question. The increased power of the Executive Branch as a whole can also be said to be a result of changes in the domestic and international environment.

Notes for this chapter appear on pages 165–166.

How does the Executive Branch respond to changes in the environment? How do particular organizations solve the problems which they face? These questions can be considered by examining issues that government organizations continually confront. Is there a problem? Can anything be done about it? Should anything be done about it? What? Who ought to do it? Consideration of these questions, stages in the process of program development, will help in understanding organizational change and problem-solving in the Executive Branch.

Is There a Problem?

Problem awareness, the feeling or judgment that the status quo is unsatisfactory, is the first step in problem-solving, the first step toward program development and change. The complexity of the problem-awareness process and the conflicts of this stage may be concealed, but they should not be underestimated. Many potential changes lapse at this stage because there may be little agreement that the status quo is unsatisfactory. For any major new program to come into existence—whether in welfare, or education, or transportation—a great number of persons must agree that the status quo is unsatisfactory. The agency or agencies directly concerned, the President and the Budget Bureau, members of Congressional committees, interest groups, all these must agree on the existence of a problem. This point deserves emphasis, because in the American pluralistic society different men often define their problems differently. Indeed, one man's problem may be the cause of another's well-being. High prices for drugs and low standards of safety and efficacy may be thought problems by the

Food and Drug Administration, some Congressmen, and some consumers, but not by other Congressmen and the industry concerned. The situation that seems to be a serious problem to one man may seem a minor problem to another, and a beneficial condition to a third. Lack of agreement on what are problems explains a good deal of government inertia.

To be sure, not all changes or new programs within the bureaucracy require the same degree of support and agreement. Bureaucratic agencies may change their regulations after no more than a public hearing; and the President may issue executive orders that require only Congressional acquiesence, if that. But before there is change, the status quo must be viewed as unsatisfactory by enough of the relevant participants. (The definitions of "enough" and "relevant" depend of course on what is at stake.)

How do bureaucratic organizations become aware of problems or performance gaps?[1] How does dissatisfaction arise? There are numerous ways. Organizations may search for problems. Military organizations especially have intelligence units, but not only military organizations want to know what changes are taking place in the world they confront, what changes they may have to adjust to.[2] The Census Bureau, the Bureau of Labor Statistics, and the Office of Education are all examples of organizations that collect information to identify problems and provide a basis for program changes. Other government organizations may use this information and may collect their own more specialized information. The FBI's statistics on crime are famous.

Besides collecting external data, bureaucratic organizations may also collect internal data on their own performance, and this may result in proposals for change. Any particular agency may be in contact with

agencies (federal, state, foreign, or private) doing similar work, with professional societies, and with a clientele
of various types—and all these contacts may bring in
information that may identify problems and lead to
change proposals. Many government agencies are of
course engaged in scientific research and development,
the result of which may have a direct effect on what
they propose and do.

Agency search for problems may be very limited,
and the information collected may be interpreted as
not indicative of any problems.[3] Search for problems
may be limited for a number of reasons. There may be
a shortage of resources; perhaps few funds were requested for this purpose, perhaps few were granted.
Perhaps the management of an agency thinks there are
better ways to spend money than on self-examination;
when work seems to be going smoothly, it may seem silly
to search for trouble. Management may sometimes feel
like the patient who avoids the doctor because he is
afraid of what he will be told. Optimism and a sense
of self-confidence can produce a sense of security. Even
when search does go on it may be over a limited area.
It is possible to imagine a law enforcement agency that
collects much data on crime rates, but never questions
its own organizational structure or recruiting policies.
It is possible to imagine a military organization that
collects intelligence about the enemy but does not evaluate its own performance; and it may have no intelligence about the country that unexpectedly turns out
to be an enemy. Expectations affect search. It is possible
to imagine a welfare agency that is constantly hunting
for fraud and misuse of funds but never wondering
about the overall impact of its program. It is possible
to imagine a government agency searching for information that will demonstrate that it has done and is doing
a good job.

Bureaucratic agencies may interpret what information they do obtain in a biased way. Ignorance, ideology, values, and self-interest may all affect the interpretation of information. Data on Soviet military capabilities may be interpreted by the Pentagon in such a way as to suggest the need for greater military might. A budget analyst or Congressman may look at the same information and think American capabilities quite sufficient. Data on crime rates may be interpreted by police to mean that more police are needed; others may look at the same data and conclude that the present system is a failure and scrapping it might make as much sense as enlarging it. It is hard for organizations to admit that what they are doing is wrong or irrelevant or that their performance is simply inadequate, and this fact may affect their interpretation of information. Sometimes agencies may get information that they do not understand or whose significance they do not appreciate. They may get conflicting information or information that lends itself to multiple interpretations. Facts must be given meaning, and different people and organizations may give the same facts different meanings.

Limited search and biased interpretation may both interfere with problem awareness. But in our pluralistic political system and indeed in our pluralistic Executive Branch many actors or participants initially may become aware of problems and call them to the attention of relevant agencies and political officials. In any particular policy area there may be several agencies, and the problems not found by one may be found by another. The Central Intelligence Agency, the Defense Intelligence Agency, the National Security Agency, and the individual services all collect intelligence. The Bureau of the Census and the Bureau of Labor Statistics both collect socioeconomic statistics, as do other agencies. Several other examples of groups of cooperating (and competing) agencies could be given. Although these kinds of groupings may raise visions of duplication and overlapping, it is well to remember that the policy field in the hands of one agency may contain unexposed problems. The draft, in the hands solely of the Selective Service System, is a case that comes to mind. But the Selective Service System and the recent debates about the draft also demonstrate that problems can be brought to the surface by Congressmen, Presidential commissions, journalists, and a wide variety of intellectuals. In a pluralistic political system, the search activities of bureaucratic agencies are supplemented in many ways.

For new programs or other sorts of changes to come about it is not enough that only one participant identify a problem; a number of participants must agree that a problem exists. Such agreement may be difficult to reach. Admitting the existence of a problem—malnutrition in rural areas, increasing rates of illegitimacy, disproportionate draft deferment of upper income youths —may have political repercussions, and the existing pattern of social benefits and burdens may be disturbed. Achieving agreement on the existence of a problem may require an educational effort. Officials, to say nothing of the public, may just be unable to interpret statistical data; or the data revealing a problem may conflict with their preferences, values, or habits. Reaction to the data on the health effects of smoking is an example. Achieving agreement that a problem exists may take time, perhaps years; but agreement can be hurried by a crisis. Senator Kefauver thought the regulation of drugs too lax, but it took deformed babies to concern enough people to support him.[4] It took assassinations to convince enough people that uncontrolled trade in firearms was a problem. Agreement may also be hurried when a visible, influential figure (the President, for example) becomes convinced and starts convincing others. When wide agreement that a problem exists is reached, the next stage of the change process begins.

Can Anything Be Done?

There is a difference between being convinced that a particular condition is a problem and being able to do anything about it. There may not be enough knowledge to carry out a solution: It is possible with available knowledge to virtually wipe out mosquitoes and malaria; but it is not possible now to wipe out cancer, though of course it is possible to carry on a research program that could lead to an eradication program. There also may not be enough money or skilled manpower to carry out a program, or using these resources to solve one problem may prevent the solution of another. The proposed solution may be worse than the problem. Solutions to some social problems may be impossible legally and politically, assuming more or less durable cultural values and political preferences. It may be difficult, however, for agencies and officials (to say nothing of politicians) to admit that a problem is insoluble. If the problem is obvious, doing anything may be passed off as a solution.[5] Under the "anything is better than nothing" assumption, physicians used to bleed ill patients; medicine, at least, has advanced since those days.

At any one time there are likely to be more problems than resources for solutions. What kinds of problems are selected for solution? The ones that attract the interest of influential participants, those in which there appears to be the most popular interest, causes of crisis, and those that can be solved cheaply. These several

criteria may mean that some problems—like water pollution—may wait a long time. They are not dramatic, and
effective solution may be expensive. Perhaps it is more
useful to ask about a problem not whether anything
can be done about it, but whether anything can be done
now.

Related to the question, "Can anything be done?,"
is another question: "Should anything be done?" Information, ideology, and self-interest may all affect the
answer. Those likely to be affected detrimentally by
action may argue that nothing should be done, and they
may also argue publicly that nothing can be done. General Lewis B. Hershey, for many years the Director of
the Selective Service System, would admit grudgingly
that the draft was unfair, but add that life itself was
unfair. He would admit variation among local boards,
but also point out variation among judges and juries.
In short he would admit some problems, but imply that
nothing could be done about them.[6] But if some participants argue that nothing can or should be done about
a particular problem others will argue that something
not only can be done, but must be done. For change in
the status quo to take place there has to be substantial
agreement that something can and ought to be done.

What Ought to be Done and
Who Ought to Do It?

Once there is agreement to solve a problem, attention turns to what and how and who. At this stage in
the program development process alternative solutions
to problems are proposed and evaluated. There may be
wide agreement that institutions of higher education
are in financial trouble, but is the solution to be federal

grants to institutions, scholarships or loans to students, or tax benefits to parents? All these proposals are plausible and debatable alternatives. There may be widespread agreement that crimes of violence are a serious and growing problem, but what can and ought to be done? Should there be a national police force, or should state and local forces be strengthened and improved and if so, how? Or do we know enough to do anything? Should unskilled unemployed young men be given job training in their own communities, or should they leave their community for a center where they can learn new skills and new behavior patterns in a new environment? Transportation in urban areas is a problem, but is the answer mass transit or more expressways? The point is clear. Virtually any problem has several possible solutions, though any advocate may argue that there is really only one.

Naturally, alternatives often vary in their cost, effectiveness, and political acceptability, though the magnitude of these variables may be hazy. Program debates are notable for producing opinions, judgments, and conclusions, not facts. The effectiveness of proposed solutions may be especially unclear. Proposed programs resemble in some ways untested though plausible hypotheses. Advocates, however, are likely to express confidence that what they favor will work. However, certain participants in a policy debate may not want a problem solved, or think there is no problem. In such a case it may appear to them wiser not to say this openly, but instead to propose a course of action that they think will not affect the status quo.

Just as there are alternative solutions to problems there are alternative ways to implement solutions. Within the Executive Branch there are many groups of agencies in the same policy areas. Thus several agencies may be able to carry out a program. Presumably the FBI could protect the President, the Department of Interior could manage the nation's forests, and the Maritime Administration could be in the Department of Transportation. But in fact the Secret Service (located not in the Department of Justice but in the Treasury) protects the President, the Forest Service is in the Department of Agriculture, and the Maritime Administration is in the Department of Commerce.

Rather than giving responsibility for a new program to an existing agency it is possible (and not uncommon) to create a new agency. The National Aeronautics and Space Administration was created to manage the space program of the nation; the Office of Economic Opportunity was created to oversee a War on Poverty. Sometimes a new agency is created because no appropriate agency exists; more often new agencies are created to carry out new programs that existing agencies may not handle well. NASA was created to avoid military dominance of the space program, and the Atomic Energy Commission was created after World War II to give civilian control to the nuclear energy program.

The answer to how a program should be administered or a problem solved need not involve the federal bureaucracy exclusively or at all. In the United States federal system, the states often carry out programs. The grant-in-aid in its various forms has long provided federal money to the states. For highways, health, welfare, and education, federal funds have been used to support programs administered largely by the states, though with federal conditions and federal supervision. The Bureau of Public Roads has worked with state highway departments in the construction of the interstate highway system, the Office of Education has worked with state departments of education, the Welfare Administration has worked with state departments of welfare. In a sense the state bureaucracies become extensions of the federal bureaucracy. If this were not possible the federal bureaucracy might be much larger. Even when grants-in-aid are not involved, the states may be heavily involved in carrying out federal programs such as the National Guard and the Selective Service System.

Another way of carrying out a program without substantially increasing the size of the federal bureaucracy is to contract for service with a private corporation or other nongovernmental organization. Today much government research and development, construction, and supplies and equipment come from contractors. The Defense Department relies heavily on the services of contractors, and NASA has played the role of supervisor to hundreds of contractors and subcontractors.

Voluntary action or voluntary compliance by citizens may be suggested as an alternative to government action. This alternative was suggested by the automobile industry before the Traffic Safety Act was passed to develop mandatory automobile safety standards. An alternative suggested by many as a replacement for the draft is voluntary enlistment. Sometimes voluntary action will be undependable or insufficient, but for some reason direct government action may appear unsatisfactory. In such cases the tax system of the government may be used to elicit or reward certain kinds of behavior. Thus, rather than receiving direct grants or direct payments, a taxpayer may be given tax credits or deductions if he uses his money in certain ways. The present income tax system subsidizes an impressive array of private charities by making contributions to them tax deductible. If this were not the case, health, welfare, and education programs of the government might have to be bigger. As this is written substantial attention is being given to how the income tax system might be used to aid higher education and urban core areas.

Although in principle what will be done and who will do it are separable questions, in practice they get mixed up. What is going to be done is not unrelated to who will do it. Who will carry out a program is related to what is going to be done. If the Department of Defense were in charge of atomic energy, it would be hard to imagine much emphasis being given to civilian applications. At the early stages of any problem/policy/program debate it is likely that a number of alternative programs will be proposed together with appropriate administrative arrangements. Existing Executive Branch agencies are likely to propose programs that they can carry out and benefit from. The White House or the Budget Bureau may suggest programs to be carried out by new or reorganized groups, and they will have their own views on how programs ought to be administered. If traditional areas of state activity (education, health, welfare, law enforcement, highways) are involved, state officials are likely to argue for state involvement. Increasingly, city officials want to bypass the state government in administering programs designed to aid cities. Business, industry, and fiscally conservative groups may want no direct government action at all but argue for tax measures that would reward private actions aimed at achieving desirable goals. Contractors who stand to benefit, as well as some Congressmen impressed with the efficiency of business organizations, may suggest that private contractors should be paid to handle the problem at hand, whether it be space engineering or job training.

A number of factors, not mutually exclusive, are likely to determine what proposals are made. Whether or not action is really desired is important. When southern Senators advocate leaving the pace of school integration to the judgment of local school officials or state authorities, it takes little imagination to know what they are after. The political, social, and economic values of policy process participants will affect what they propose. Bureaucratic self-interest is likely to be reflected in the proposals emanating from bureaucratic organizations. They tend to propose solutions they can handle, programs that they can and should administer. Relevant here is the concept of organizational ideology. Bureaucratic organizations are likely to propose solutions consistent with what they have done in the past. Brand new approaches or solutions rarely come from old-line organizations. Groups and organizations usually recommend programs and administrative arrangements they think will do them the most good or the least harm. Such factors as available resources, potential cost, and political feasibility may also affect what is proposed. Of course many organizations may engage in more or less rigorous and objective analysis of the possible consequences, costs, and benefits of alternative programs and develop their proposals accordingly; their final proposals depend on both the results of their analysis and their own goals. Just as program proposals resemble untested hypotheses, so do suggested administrative arrangements. The normal assumption is that what is proposed will work, but often this assumption rests on no strong evidence. In contrast to the testing of scientific hypotheses, programs and their administration are not often rigorously tested or discarded if they do not work.

The Final Choice

After alternative actions are evaluated, choice follows. In a sense no choice is final. Decisions made one year may be modified the next. Still it is useful to think of the last step of program development as the choice. How and where is this step taken? What considerations are likely to affect it? Are there any general similarities among final choices?

The mythology of American government has it that final program choices are made when Congress votes, or maybe when the President signs a bill. This is only occasionally true. American government contains many decision-makers, and any one of them, depending on the circumstances, may make the final choice. As we know, legislation may be initiated in an Executive Branch agency and be virtually rubber-stamped all along the legislative line until it comes back to the agency for implementation. Programs may be developed by the White House, the Budget Bureau, special task forces, or interest groups. If we discard the idea of formal choice and look instead for the meaningful choice, we may more easily see that there is no single location for choosing. Who has the last word may depend on a variety of things: the problem at hand, the proposed solutions, the groups that may be affected, the agencies concerned, the abilities and interests of their heads, the party in power—both in the White House and in Congress—and the interests and abilities of the President.

Because in our political system there are so many people who might have the last word, who in fact does have it may not be clear, and appearances may be misleading. When events turn out well there is no shortage of men who will claim responsibility and credit; when they turn out poorly it may be hard to find out who to debit. Was the decision made in an agency by some invisible bureaucrat, or was it made by the Secretary of the department? Was it made in the Budget Bureau or by a White House staffer or by the President himself? Did the chairman of a Congressional committee exercise an informal but very real veto? The answers to such questions require research, not resource to organization charts and the Constitution. A thorough investigation into a particular program or decision may conclude that it is impossible to tell just who made what decisions.

Much important executive decision-making is unpublicized and takes place in confidential meetings. For the bureaucracy there is nothing resembling either the *Congressional Record* or the *Congressional quarterly*. The sheer volume of decision-making in the Executive Branch makes it even more difficult to follow. Of course, inaction is also a form of choice. Proposals may not be made by agencies, ideas may be pigeon-holed in the White House, and bills in Congress may languish in committee. Further, all these inactions may go unpublicized.

For a program to be effective, consistent choices or decisions have to be made in three areas. A program has to be authorized, funded, and given to an appropriate agency for implementation. Yet these choices are not always consistent. A program may be authorized, but not funded; or it may be authorized but put in the hands of an organization that will not administer it properly. Why do such things occur? A program which has been authorized may not be funded because authorization and funding are done by separate Congressional committees which may not see eye-to-eye on the need for a program. There is another explanation for inconsistencies in program-budget organization. Authorizing a program with some fanfare may satisfy one group; not funding it or funding it at a low level may mollify another. Passing a law may apparently gain votes in one place; giving it to an agency that will not enforce it or giving the agency so little money that it cannot enforce it may gain votes in another place.

In short, program development and change frequently cause conflict among various policy process participants with different interests. Some participants may for a variety of reasons resist any change in the status quo. Perhaps they are benefiting from the status quo; perhaps they fear any change would leave them worse off than before; perhaps they don't want the government to spend more money. Other participants may desire change in the status quo, but this group may be divided into several more with each proposing a different course of action. Given this kind of conflict the status quo is likely to remain unchanged. The status quo is likely to continue until a sufficiently large coalition has not only agreed on the need for change, but also agreed on an alternative. The first part, agreement on the need for change, is hardly simple. It is not enough that people regard the status quo as not ideal; rather they must regard it as unacceptable and they must be willing to pay a price for change. This last condition is an obstacle to many programs, and to a good deal of change. Often the price that people are willing to pay will not purchase very much change in the status quo. Of course if they are willing to pay repeatedly, as on the installment plan, a good deal of change may occur over time. Agreement on a particular alternative may be even harder to achieve than agreement on the need for change. It may not be reached until proponents of various alternatives are convinced that virtually anything would be better than the status quo. As long as different groups support uncompromisingly their particular positions the status quo is likely to continue. As we have noted earlier it may take a crisis to precipitate action.

To this discussion should be added the obvious notion that some kinds of changes are easier than others. The fewer people that must agree, the easier change will be. A change that apparently affects only a few people may be easier than one that affects many. Changes with apparently predictable consequences may be easier than changes whose possible results are unknown. A change that appears as almost no change at all is likely to be easier than something appearing revolutionary. In effect little changes are easier than big changes. And they are more common. In American government much change, much program development, is marginal, incremental. Big changes are infrequent and unlikely.[7] Perhaps they are not often possible in a pluralistic and participative political system.

Notes for Chapter 6

1. The phrase, *performance gap*, is taken from Anthony Downs, *Inside Bureaucracy* (Boston: Little, Brown and Co., 1967), p. 191.

2. A relevant and very interesting book is Harold L. Wilensky, *Organizational Intelligence* (New York: Basic Books, 1967).

3. An example is the Selective Service System. See James W. Davis, Jr. and Kenneth M. Dolbeare, *Little Groups of Neighbors* (Chicago: Markham Publishers, 1968).

4. The reference is to the thalidomide scare in the early 1960s.

5. Relevant here is Murray Edelman's book, *The Sym-*

bolic Uses of Politics (Urbana: University of Illinois Press, 1964).

6. See for example General Hershey's testimony before the Committee on Armed Services, U.S. House of Representatives, *Review of the Administration and Operation of the Selective Service System,* Hearings, (89th Congress, 2nd session, June 22–24, 28–30, 1966).

7. See the work of Charles Lindblom, especially his "The Science of Muddling Through," *Public Administration Review* 19 (1959), pp. 70–88.

★★★★
★★★

THE BUDGETING
PROCESS

WHAT THE GOVERNMENT does and how much it spends are closely related; programs and budgets are inextricably linked. The plans of a President and the programs of Executive Branch agencies are nothing without funds. A civil rights law with no organization to enforce it—and this takes money—is law only on the books. The many programs of the war on poverty are nothing without money; they are merely paper programs. To reduce crime and rehabilitate criminals, to preserve natural resources, to provide a transportation system— all these activities take money. It is the President's budget that allocates funds among the many and varied programs of the federal government. The budget can

Notes for this chapter appear on pages 192–193.

be viewed as an expression of priorities, preferences, and values. It converts hopes and symbols into realities. Lip service may be given by Congressmen and Presidents to many things; the budget shows what they are really willing to support.

The Preparation of the Federal Budget

Each year in January the President of the United States sends his budget and his budget message to the Congress. This event represents the culmination of many months of work in the Executive Branch, months of evaluation, calculation, and negotiation. The basic outline of the process has been described at length by the Bureau of the Budget, and it may be useful to quote their description before considering some particular aspects of the budgetary process in more detail.[1]

> The preparation of the Federal budget for any fiscal year covers at least 18 months. Thus, each spring attention is directed to the planning of programs for the next fiscal year, which will begin the next July; and to the development of preliminary plans and policies for the succeeding fiscal year. Even during the period of specific work on a particular budget, attention is also given to projecting the effect of program decisions on subsequent budgets and to identifying major issues or problems affecting the budget in the future.
>
> The procedure changes somewhat from year to year, depending on administrative situation and current conditions. Currently, for example, efforts are being made to refine existing and develop new planning and programming techniques and to integrate them more closely with the budget process. The results of these efforts should become a significant factor in the budget process in the future.

PRELIMINARY STEPS

Under the newly established integrated planning-pro-
gramming-budgeting system each major agency will,
around the 1st of May, submit to the Bureau of the
Budget its program and financial plan which expresses
in financial and nonfinancial quantitative terms the
goals, objectives, and planned accomplishments for the
next several fiscal years, usually five. The plan is a
comprehensive document covering all the activities of
the agency and dividing such activities into output
oriented program categories; i.e., categories which
reflect what is to be accomplished by each program.
It reflects the agency head's judgment on what should
be the agency's future course of action to meet the
Nation's needs with which his agency is concerned.

The latest approved plan is accompanied by a program memorandum, setting forth analyses of the programming, possible alternative goals, and alternative
methods for achieving them. Techniques such as cost
analysis, operations research, and cost benefit analysis
are utilized in the agency to assist in arriving and
supporting the recommendations and alternatives set
forth in the program memorandum.

The agency submissions are subjected to a critical
examination in late May or June by Bureau of the
Budget examiners who are assigned continuing responsibility with respect to agency programs. The
issues, agency program plans, and the examiners
recommendations are discussed with the Director of
the Bureau of the Budget. During the entire process
efforts are made by the agencies and by the Bureau
to weed out marginal and obsolete activities so that
resources may be shifted to more essential activities.

After the Bureau review is complete, Bureau recommendations on the plans and issues are discussed
with the President. When the President has reviewed
the recommendations, the agency head is notified,
and usually the Director meets with him to discuss

the effect of the review process on the agency's programs. Agency program plans are also updated to reflect the results of this process.

Concurrent with preparation of program and financial plans in the agencies, staff of the Bureau of the Budget, in cooperation with staff of the Treasury Department and the Council of Economic Advisors, review the long range effect of agency programs on the fiscal guidelines set forth in the latest budget. They develop tentative assumptions on the economic environment which may govern the preparation of future budgets, and make projections of revenues to be expected under these assumptions. The budgetary outlook is discussed with the President and sometimes with the Cabinet.

After the review of the agency program plans by the Bureau of the Budget preliminary estimates of their effect on fiscal requirements are developed. The Director recommends the fiscal policies to be followed in preparing the budget, as discussed and agreed to by the Secretary of the Treasury and the Chairman of the Council of Economic Advisors. The President's decision as to policies are communicated to the heads of the various agencies within the executive branch for their guidance in preparing their budgets.

COMPILATION AND SUBMISSION OF AGENCY ESTIMATES
During the next several months agencies compile the detailed schedules and supporting information in accordance with the instructions prescribed by the Bureau of the Budget (Circular No. A-11).

The process of compiling the detailed estimates begins with the personnel who are responsible for carrying out the actual operations and these estimates are reviewed at various levels in each agency. At each level of review, of course, the view point is different—the regional office must consider the estimates of each field station in relation to other field stations and to the total requirements for the region. Finally, at the departmental level, the estimates for bureaus and major programs must be judged in comparison with other bureaus and programs and with the total for the agency.

Agency budget submissions are due in the Bureau of the Budget in September. In order that the budget document may reflect the complete situation, the submission covers all accounts in which money is available for obligation or expenditure, whether or not any action by Congress is requested. The submissions reflect amounts specifically requested for the budget year for continuing activities being carried on at the date of the budget submission, as well as for items "proposed for separate transmittal," covering anticipated additional requirements for both the current and budget years which are foreseeable at that time.

REVIEW OF THE AGENCY ESTIMATES IN THE
BUREAU OF THE BUDGET

When the estimates are received in the Bureau of the Budget, they are referred to the examiners assigned to the programs involved. The examiners must be thoroughly familiar with the President's budget policy and previous congressional action, as well as with the programs of the agency and their relationship to activities of other agencies. The examiners at this time give considerable attention to the basis for the individual estimates—the volume of work on hand and forecast; the method by which the agency proposes to accomplish its objectives; and the estimates of requirements in terms of numbers of people. They review past performance, check the accuracy of factual information presented, and consider the future implications of the program. They identify matters of major importance and the issues involved for discussion with agency representatives at hearings.

After the hearings are completed, the examiners

prepare their recommendations for the Director's review. This review concentrates attention principally on the major items involving Presidential policy, but also provides a test check on other aspects of the recommendations. Assumptions with respect to the economic outlook and the international situation are brought up to date as a basis for this review.

Examining staff sometimes discuss the Director's tentative decisions with the budget officer of the agency to identify and narrow the issues which require detailed Presidential attention.

The process of review occupies the Bureau of the Budget from the latter part of September until the beginning of December. During this period, the economic outlook is again assessed by the Treasury Department, the Council of Economic Advisors, and the Bureau, and revenue estimates are jointly agreed to for presentation to the President.

DECISION BY THE PRESIDENT

As portions of the Budget Bureau review are completed, tables and analyses are prepared to present the Director's recommendations to the President, identifying the issues involved. The problem of recommending programs which will meet the most urgent needs of the country, and still be prudent within the constraint imposed by the availability of resources, is complicated by the large segment of budget expenditures which is relatively unaffected by the budget process—for the last few years such items as interest on the public debt, veterans pensions, grants for public assistance, and agricultural price support have accounted for over half of the total budget expenditures other than the national defense items, or about 25 per cent of the grand total. The level of these expenditures depends upon provisions of the laws which authorized the program and on other factors not readily subject to annual budgetary control. As soon as the President makes his decisions on programs and fiscal policies, each agency is notified of these decisions, including the amounts allowed for that agency. Occasionally an agency appeals (through the Director) to obtain an upward revision of the allowance. Final decision depends on the President's position in the matter.

PREPARATION OF THE BUDGET DOCUMENT

When the agency receives its budget allowance, the estimates are revised to conform with the President's decisions for inclusion in the printed budget documents.

As soon as revision of the individual schedules for each agency are completed, the figures from the individual appropriation and authorization schedules are summarized for each agency. Figures from the agency summaries are then consolidated to make up the tables which, together with final revenue estimates prepared by the Treasury Department, set forth the budget totals.

When the budget is finally in order and the budget message is written, they are transmitted to the Congress in the January preceding the start of the fiscal year. The budget is considered in detail first by the House of Representatives Appropriations Committee and by the House as a whole and then by the Senate Appropriations Committee and the Senate. Ideally Congressional action on the budget is completed by the start of the fiscal year, July 1. But often action is not completed, forcing agencies to operate with continuing resolutions (Congressional authorizations to operate at the same level as in the preceding year) until action can be completed.

Programs and Budgets: Some
Recent Developments

The description of the preparation of the federal budget by the Bureau of the Budget emphasized the relationship between agency programs and agency budgets. Although programs and budgets have always been linked, the linkage has not always been so explicit as in recent years. Indeed, not many years ago it was impossible to tell by looking at the government budget how much money was being allocated to particular programs. One could find out how much was spent on salaries, on telephone calls, or on automobiles, but not how much was spent on each program of the government. During the 1930s, however, the Department of Agriculture and the Tennessee Valley Authority began to classify their budgets on a program basis; and other organizations followed their lead during World War II. After the war the First Hoover Commission recommended in its report[2] on budgeting and accounting that "the whole budgetary concept of the Federal Government should be refashioned by the adoption of a budget based on functions, activities, and projects: this we designate a 'performance budget.'" Further encouragement to program budgeting came from the National Security Act of 1949, the Budget and Accounting Procedures Act of 1950, and the Second Hoover Commission.

Yet in 1960 it was clear that the linkage between programs and budgets was not as explicit as it might be. For example the Defense Department budget allocated resources to: Military Personnel, Operation and Maintenance; Procurement; Military Construction; and Research, Development, Test, and Evaluation. As one critic said, "From the point of view of relating the budget to national strategy, this arrangement has little apparent advantage over the old one."[3]

As well as budgets that were less than revealing about programs, economists saw other difficulties with government budgeting in the 1950s. Consideration of the budget was on an agency-by-agency basis, even though several agencies might be doing complementary or even contradictory things. For example, funds spent on natural resources in the Department of Interior were considered apart from funds devoted to natural resources in the Department of Agriculture. Moreover, budgeting was on an annual basis with little systematic thought given to the future financial implications of currently proposed projects.

All this began to change with the publication in 1960 of a book by Charles J. Hitch and Roland N. McKean (*The Economics of Defense in the Nuclear Age*[4]) and the entrance of Robert McNamara into the Department of Defense. The ideas on budgeting that Hitch had propounded in his book began to be introduced in the Defense Department. It is worthwhile taking time to look at these ideas, because they have since been extended to the rest of the Executive Branch.

First, funds began to be explicitly allocated to the various programs of the armed forces. These programs (or *missions*, as they were called) are listed below.[5]

PROGRAM I

Strategic Retaliatory Forces: the forces that are designed to carry out the long-range strategic mission and to carry the main burden of battle in general. They include the long-range bombers, the air to ground and decoy missiles, and the refueling tankers; the land based and submarine based strategic missiles; and the systems for their command and control.

PROGRAM II

Continental Air and Missile Defense Forces: those weapon systems, warning and communications networks and ancillary equipment required to detect, identify, track, and destroy unfriendly forces approaching the North American continent.

PROGRAM III

General Purpose Forces: the forces relied upon to perform the entire range of combat operations short of general nuclear war. These include most of the Army's combat and combat support units, virtually all Navy units, all Marine Corps units, and the tactical units of the Air Force.

PROGRAM IV

Airlift and Sealift Forces: those airlift and sealift forces required to move troops and cargo promptly to wherever they might be needed. Included in the airlift forces are both MATS transports and the Air Force Tactical Air Command troop carrier aircraft. The sealift forces include the troop ships, cargo ships, and tankers operated by MSTS and the "Forward Floating Bases."

PROGRAM V

Reserve and National Guard Forces: equipment, training, and administration of the Reserve and National Guard personnel of the several services.

PROGRAM VI

Research and Development: all research and development effort not directly identified with elements of other programs (i.e., where there has been no decision to produce the inventory).

PROGRAM VII

General Support: support activities of the several services and the agencies that serve the entire Department of Defense. It constitutes an "all-other" or residual category of activities or programs and includes all costs not capable of being directly or meaningfully allocated to the other major programs.

PROGRAM VIII
Military Assistance: equipment, training, and related services provided for armed forces of allied and friendly nations.

PROGRAM IX
Civil Defense: federal assistance for fallout, shelters, warning and radiological monitoring systems, training and education for emergency preparedness, etc.

These budget categories are markedly different from the budget categories used during the 1950s. (The 1950s categories are still in use, but they are not the only categories.) An important feature of the new categories is that they are not limited to particular services. All services contribute to the strategic retaliatory force, all services contribute to the general-purpose forces, and so on. By in effect pooling service contributions, the total level of resources being allocated to one mission or another can be seen.

A second feature of the new defense budgeting system was that more attention was given explicitly to the analysis of alternative ways of achieving the same goal. Secretary McNamara required the military departments to be explicit about what they wanted to accomplish and to justify the route they had chosen to reach their objectives. The form of analysis he most emphasized has been called many things—cost-benefit analysis, cost-effectiveness analysis, cost-utility analysis. Cost-benefit analysis is the term that will be used in this account.

The cost-benefit analyst arrays in front of himself a number of ways to accomplish the task he is concerned with—a variety of fighter bombers to provide close support for ground troops, approaches to the problems of unemployed urban youth, or ways to transport people in urban areas. The analyst then must find out which alternative will provide the most benefit for the least cost. He may start with a given number of dollars and see which alternative will give him the most return for his money. Or he may start with a particular goal and see what alternative will reach that goal with the fewest dollars.

A third component of the budgeting system that was introduced into the Department of Defense was long-range financial planning. Budget officers were required to think ahead five years and make clear what they thought their requirements would be during that period. Their current requests could then be assessed not only in the light of what they had spent in the past but what they anticipated spending in the future. Budget officers were required to be explicit about the future cost implications of current outlays. If a research and development laboratory is built this year, it will have to be staffed and maintained in future years. How much will this cost? If a contract is let this year to design a new reconnaissance plane, how much will building it cost? These questions began to be asked in the early 1960s.

The new budgeting system in the Department of Defense came to be known, as most things are in Washington, by a set of initials—PPBS, for Planning, Programming, Budgeting System. From the Defense Department, PPBS spread over the rest of the federal agencies.[6]

> In May 1966 all departments and most agencies of the U.S. Government, in submitting to the Budget Bureau their rough spending plans for the fiscal year starting fourteen months later, began using for the

first time the Planning, Programming, Budgeting System, or PPBS. The change has its source in the summer of 1965, when Lyndon B. Johnson ordered them to institute what he called a "revolutionary" new system, one which demands that departments and agencies define clearly the major objectives (or "programs") which they choose to pursue, that they apply systematic analyses to the alternative ways in which these objectives are being—or may be—sought, and that they plan their spending in long range as well as one-year ahead terms.

As soon as PPBS began to be introduced in civilian agencies, a number of problems presented themselves. One problem quickly apparent was a lack of data that prevented the analysis and evaluation of programs. Elizabeth Drew has made the problem clear:[7]

> Those who picture Washington as one mass of files and computers containing more information than they would like will be comforted by the experiences of program planners in attempting to evaluate on-going programs. Whatever the files and computers do contain, there is precious little in them about how many and whom the programs are reaching, and whether they are doing what they are supposed to do. If the purpose of an adult basic education program is to teach people how to read and write, the Office of Education might reasonably be expected to know how many people thereby actually learned how to read and write, but it does not. The higher education study was delayed because there simply was too little information about who was receiving federal scholarships, or what happened to all those who had been receiving National Defense Education Act loans since 1958. Did they finish college? Did it affect their subsequent careers? No answers. The Public Health Service might be expected to know whether its various

health services are in fact making people healthier, but it does not. The study of disease control was to have encompassed more diseases, but so little was known about the effective treatment of alcoholism and heart disease that these components had to be dropped. Those working on the income maintenance study found that the Welfare Administration could not tell them very much about the public assistance case-load—who was on welfare, where did they come from, why were they on it, what they needed in order to get off.

These gaps in information and cost data could, of course, be filled, and presumably have been. That they needed filling in 1966 when PPBS was begun in HEW testifies to a long-standing analysis gap in American public policy. But other difficulties could not be easily remedied. One obvious problem is the conceptualization and measurement of benefits. Is a scenic highway right-of-way better than a dull highway right-of-way? How much better? Do workers work better in an air-conditioned building than in one that is not air-conditioned? Certainly. How do you know, and how can you prove it? Do they work better enough to justify the cost? Is it more beneficial to spend money for cancer research or for arthritis research? A meaningless question? Then how do you make the choice? The problems raised by the introduction of PPBS are obvious.

Another problem with PPBS is program definition. Programs consist of activities, and the analyst must decide which activities to group with one another. This is by no means an easy task, as Aaron Wildavsky has made clear.[8]

The difficulties with the program concept are illustrated in the space program. A first glance suggests that space projects are ideally suited for program budgeting because they appear as physical systems designed to accomplish different missions. Actually, there is a remarkable degree of interdependence between different missions and objectives—pride, scientific research, space exploration, military uses, etc.— so that it is impossible to apportion costs on a proper basis. Consider the problem of a rocket developed for one mission and useful for others. To apportion costs to each new mission is purely arbitrary. To allocate the cost to the first mission and regard the rocket as a free good for all subsequent missions is ludicrous. The only remotely reasonable alternative— making a separate program out of the rocket itself— does violence to the concept of programs as end projects. The difficulty is compounded because the facilities that have multiple uses like boosters and tracking networks tend to be very expensive compared to the items that are specific to a particular mission. Simple concepts of program evaporate upon inspection.

An additional problem is the matter of frankness or openness. One of the characteristics of PPBS is its emphasis on explicit statements of objectives. What are the consequences of this likely to be? Can agencies afford to be explicit, if being explicit may hinder what they are trying to do? If an objective is likely to be controversial, can an agency be expected to be clear about it? Perhaps not being explicit is a way of avoiding conflict and even accomplishing objectives. But despite all the potential risks, the Bureau of the Budget is calling for increasing clarity.

A final problem in the implementation of PPBS has been a lack of trained staff. Program evaluation and cost-benefit analysis require well-trained and imaginative personnel, men trained in economics, statistics, and mathematics. These people are in short supply, and the result is analyses and justifications that are not so well done as they might be.

With all these problems PPBS is still being applied, as the Budget Bureau description of the budget preparation process made clear. Proponents may claim less for it than they did originally, but today it is part of the Washington scene. It is still, however, the subject of much debate. Aaron Wildavsky has criticized the ignoring of political costs and has argued that political conflict will be intensified when goals are made explicit. To these charges can be added the fear that PPBS will result in increased centralization.[9] "As presently conceived, program budgeting contains an extreme centralizing bias. Power is to be centralized in the Presidency (through the Budget Bureau) at the national level, in superdepartments rather than bureaus within the executive branch, and in the Federal government as a whole instead of State or local governments." William Capron, on the other hand, has argued that PPBS can in fact lead to decentralization.[10] But even he admits, agreeing with Wildavsky, that PPBS may lead to reorganization, as the organizational structure is made more congruent (it will never be completely congruent) with the program structure. The recent creation of the Department of Transportation is an example of the organizational impact of PPBS. The Bureau of the Budget itself has even been reorganized in order better to cope with the demands of program analysis.

The most important question, however, is not what effect PPBS will have on the structure of the government, but rather what effect will it have on budgetary decisions. We will take up this question after we have considered the politics of budgeting.

Politics and Budgets

The discussion so far may have left the erroneous impression that budgeting is mainly a rational analytical process. On the contrary, it is useful to remember the title of Professor Lasswell's classic book, *Politics: Who Gets What, When, How?* Budgetary decisions clearly are decisions about who gets what. Just as certainly they are infused with politics. What does this mean? It means that budgets are the result of bargaining and negotiation, and that any annual budget represents in some sense a compromise between what an agency started out to get and what other decision-makers thought it ought to have.

It is important to know who the principals are in this politics of budgeting. First are the bureaus and departments and the independent agencies, the units that make the initial requests and who finally spend the money. Then come the Bureau of the Budget and the President; they evaluate requests and make recommendations. The Bureau of the Budget makes recommendations to the President, the President makes recommendations to the Congress. The House and Senate Appropriations Committees are the third set of participants.

Each of these participants has different interests and faces different problems in the budgeting process. Bureaus, departments, and independent agencies have to decide initially how much money they want. Departments must review bureau budgets and prepare departmental budgets. They therefore must allocate funds among their bureaus. The Bureau of the Budget must formulate initial guidelines, and make final recommendations to the President. In each case its problem is to decide how much each organization should get. The President in turn must decide how much to ask from Congress. Like the Bureau of the Budget and the President, the Congress—more especially the House and Senate Appropriations Committees—must decide how much to give each agency. They must decide whether to accept the President's recommendations or to change them. The Senate must decide how to react to the action of the House.

This list of questions gives some notion of the questions that the participants in the budgeting process face. How do they arrive at their decisions? Aaron Wildavsky's book, *The Politics of the Budgetary Process*, provides a valuable discussion; and the paragraphs that follow lean heavily on this source.[11]

Agencies usually try to increase their budgets. They are not always successful, and some may not even try; but agencies each year are likely to ask for somewhat more than the year before. If an agency is to keep the confidence of the appropriations subcommittee that deals with it, its request for funds must appear reasonable in the light of past increases. Agency officials know that increases are likely to be scrutinized, and a noticeably larger increase will receive a thorough going-over. However, neither is an agency likely to ask for a bare-bones budget with no slack in it. Administrators do not like to admit budget padding, but it is certainly true that the programs in a budget may vary in importance; if cuts have to be made, some programs can be cut more easily than others. Even though Congress (and some citizens) may have a different opinion, from the administrator's point of view it makes sense to build slack into a budget. It not only protects him from the consequences of congressional action, but it also provides him with operating flexibility throughout a fiscal year.

An agency is likely to decide how much to ask for by looking to its past. With the amount it received last year as the base, it will probably try for as big an increase as it obtained then. The best predictor of the size of next year's budget is the size of this year's. Yet the past is not all that an agency attends to in deciding how much to request. An agency receives guidelines from the Bureau of the Budget; and certainly these are considered, though perhaps not followed. Officials of the administration may make public speeches indicating interest in one or another area of public policy, and these expressions of interest may be taken as hints of support by agency officials when a budget is drawn up. If the President shows interest in oceanography and a willingness to support it, this cue is not likely to pass unnoticed in the Environmental Science Services Administration or in the Office of Naval Research. If an influential Congressman indicates a willingness to support a particular activity, this fact may be reflected in an agency budget.

No matter how conscientious an agency, when a budget comes under the scrutiny of the Bureau of the Budget it is likely to be cut. Surely the Bureau of the Budget does not cut indiscriminately (though it has been charged with cutting arbitrarily), and sometimes it may not cut at all, but it does cut frequently. Any particular action depends heavily on the guidance the bureau receives from the President. Just as the agencies search for clues that might indicate Presidential support, so does the Bureau. Is the President interested in education, in urban housing problems, in traffic safety? Then programs in these areas may be generously funded. Is the President disinterested in antitrust activity or the shipping industry? Then programs in these areas may

But the Bureau does not look only to the President for guidance. It is also likely to be influenced by the receive critical scrutiny.

past actions of the Congress and indeed may model its decisions along the lines of past Congressional decisions. Has Congress been generous with the National Institutes of Health? Then the Bureau may be generous also if only because it does not want to diminish its influence (tarnish its image) by being reversed. Has Congress been harsh with AID in past years? Then the Bureau may also be critical. There is little point in recommending funds that will almost surely not be obtained.

Besides such political considerations, the Bureau of the Budget considers other and more measurable factors. An agency's present and potential work load and associated costs may be considered, especially if the work load is readily quantifiable, as it is in the Post Office. Agency cost-benefit analyses may be reviewed to see if they support what the agency is requesting. And of course the availability of funds and the presence of competing demands may have some effect on what is recommended by the Bureau of the Budget. (The demands of Vietnam made inroads on the budgets of some domestic agencies.)

When budgets for all the agencies are finally drawn together into the President's budget, they go to the Congress. The President's budget goes first to the House Appropriations Committee, where it is divided among a number of specialized subcommittees that consider it in public hearings and closed sessions. To the hearings come administration officials who must justify their requests. Generally they find that the attitude of the subcommittee members is skeptical. The members of the Appropriations Committee in the House are usually intent on cutting the President's budget. (This may mean for any agency that its budget will be cut twice—once by the Bureau of the Budget and once more by the House Appropriations Committee.) In many instances the only real question is how large the cuts will be, but it is hard to predict what the committee and its subcommittees will do. Cuts may be arbitrary and unpredictable. At times cuts will be simply symbolic assertions of Committee authority. Sometimes a budget may not be cut at all, and sometimes more money may be added, particularly to a program that has more Congressional than Presidential sympathy.

Much scholarly attention has been paid to the hearings held by the House Appropriations subcommittees, and some comment on them may be worthwhile. In brief, administrative officials view the hearings as grueling and inherently unpredictable affairs. Interviews with bureau officials bear this out:

> There is not a bureau head here whose blood pressure doesn't go up before the appropriations hearings—even the oldest one. It's an ordeal. You don't know what questions they might ask or what case they might bring up.[12]

> Sometimes a Congressman will reach in his pocket and pull out a letter from a constituent or another Congressman, and we won't know what's coming next. Sometimes these questions don't even pertain to our estimates. And its like the man who carried his bass viol across town and never got a chance to play.[13]

Attempting to protect themselves as much as possible from adverse committee action, administrative officials may do a number of things. Certainly they may try to build a generally supportive political environment; in particular they may seek the backing of organized interest groups. But they also take care to keep their relations with their particular subcommittee in good repair. By emphasizing communication and consultation and by being frank and open, agencies try to establish a relationship of trust and confidence with their subcommittee. In addition they take appropriations hearings very seriously, preparing for them carefully and being cautious and deferential during the hearings.

> We have dress rehearsals here. I play the subcommittee chairman and we practice. I try to know what's going through their minds. . . . I conceive of myself as a football coach. I train them down here; but up on the Hill I just go and sit on the sidelines.[14]

> The bureau heads come in to talk it over, or we'll go to lunch. Then I'll say that I'm going to hold a departmental hearing strictly within the family and throw all the questions I can think of at them to see what they do with them. I throw the questions I know the Committee will ask.[15]

> For heaven's sake, rehearse. We sit around here and the division chiefs fire all the questions they can think of and I answer them. I make my whole presentation . . . you need to get a grasp of what they're going to say so you don't fumble around when the time comes. It's like boning up for a Ph.D. exam. I always know what they're going to ask and I don't think a single question has been asked that I didn't think about in advance in recent years. Ninety-five per cent of it is wasted. But that one nugget that you rehearse may make all the difference in the world.[16]

In the hearing, openness and honesty are the order of the day, and administrators say it does not pay to argue.

> The most important thing in a Committee hearing is creating an atmosphere of confidence—so that you have confidence in the Committee and they have confidence in you. I tell my people to be perfectly honest and to have a full free and frank discussion

with the Committee, even if it hurts you a little bit. That will mean more than anything else in getting your money. Nobody likes to admit things and cast reflections on his own shop, but don't try to fool the congressmen. You can't. They have a fifth sense when someone is not talking freely and frankly. If you have a perfectly open discussion, they'll have more confidence in you, and your appropriations troubles will be minimized.[17]

I like to go at things directly. I'm the kind of guy who likes to argue. But you shouldn't argue with congressmen. I learned that a long time ago.[18]

After hearings are completed the committee in closed session makes its decisions, and many agencies, try though they did, find that they received less than they requested. Ordinarily the recommendations of the subcommittees are accepted by the Appropriations Committee and also by the House. After House action, appropriations bills are sent to the Senate for consideration. Not without reason, the Senate Appropriations Committee is considered (and considers itself) the Congressional court of appeals and the court of last resort. Administrators hope that the Senate committee will restore at least some of the funds taken away by the House, and in many cases the committee obliges. A quotation from *The Politics of the Budgetary Process* is to the point.

A member of the Senate Appropriations Committee is likely to conceive of his proper role as the responsible legislator who sees to it that the irrepressible lower House does not do too much damage either to constituency or to national interests. Though members of the House Appropriations Committee tend to view their opposite members in the Senate as frivolous dilettantes who swap favors and do not care what happens to the public purse, Senators tend to reverse the compliment by regarding their brethren in the other chamber as jealous and power-hungry types who do not care what happens to "essential" programs so long as they can show that they have made cuts.[19]

After Senate action, appropriations bills often must go to a conference committee to have differences between Senate and House versions resolved. When they are resolved and the same measure is passed by both House and Senate, it goes to the President for signature.

Even from such a brief sketch of the politics of budgeting, it is clear that budgeting is hardly a rational analytical process. Rather, it seems some sort of political game with many players, each vying for different prizes. Agencies want as much money as they can get for their programs. The Bureau of the Budget wants to protect the President and tries to put together a budget that is responsive to his desires and stands a chance of getting through Congress. The House Appropriations Committee wants to economize, and the Senate Appropriations Committee wants to right the wrongs of the House Appropriations Committee. In such a context we may well inquire into the future of PPBS.

PPBS and the Political Process

Surely a safe conclusion is that politics is not going to disappear. Agencies, the Bureau of the Budget, and Congressmen are going to continue to have different views of what is proper and what is padding, different views of what is dispensable and what is vital. It is also clear that the techniques of cost-benefit analysis will be of little or no use when deciding whether to devote more money to education or highways. Moreover, although cost-benefit analysis may be relevant and useful in trying to choose between such similar social welfare programs as the Job Corps and the Neighborhood Youth Corps, it is by no means clear that the results of the analysis will be determinative. At most the results of analysis may be one more datum to be considered, but not the only one. In thinking about the impact of PPBS, it is well to remember that our values, preferences, and habits are not easily altered by mere data.

PPBS is likely to affect the terms of the budgetary argument and in some cases the budgetary decisions. A balanced analysis has come from William Capron, formerly in the Bureau of the Budget. He points out that new and different men are now involved in budgeting, the economists and systems analysts, although the politicians and accountants have not left the scene. The economists bring with them new technicians and call for new kinds of data. As Capron puts it, "The ethos of budgeting will shift from justification to analysis. To a far greater extent than heretofore, budget decisions will be influenced by explicit statements of objectives and by a formal weighing of the costs and benefits of alternatives."[20] But he does not go a great deal further in asserting three claims for PPBS.

> —the dialogue between the parties involved (the bureaus, the departments, the Executive Office of the President, the Congress, the private interest groups and "constituencies" will be conducted differently and will certainly be "impacted" by PPBS.
> —some decisions will be different from what they otherwise would be without this approach.
> —and some of these decisions will be better than they would have been, absent the use of more formalized analysis.

Although budget and program are being subjected to more analysis than ever, politics—negotiation, bargaining, and compromise—will continue to play important roles in the budget process.

Notes for Chapter 7

1. Material submitted by Bureau of the Budget at Hearings Before the Committee on Appropriations, House of Representatives, 89th Congress, 2nd session, January 31, 1966, pp. 66–67.

2. Quoted in Arthur Smithies, "Conceptual Framework for the Program Budget," in David Novick (ed.), *Program Budgeting* (Washington: U.S.G.P.O., 1965), p. 7.

3. Smithies, "Conceptual Framework," p. 9.

4. Charles J. Hitch and Roland N. McKean, *The Economics of Defense in the Nuclear Age* (New York: Atheneum, 1965). Originally published by the Harvard University Press.

5. Taken from David Novick, "The Department of Defense," in Novick, *Program Budgeting*, pp. 59–60. Novick excerpted the material from a statement by Secretary of Defense Robert S. McNamara before the Committee on Armed Services on the Fiscal Year 1965–1966 Defense Program and 1965 Defense Budget, January 27, 1964, Hearings on Military Posture and H.R. 9637, House of Representatives, 88th Congress, 2nd session (Washington: U.S.G.P.O., 1964).

6. Virginia Held, "PPBS Comes to Washington," *Public Interest,* Summer 1966, p. 102.

7. Elizabeth Drew, "HEW Grapples With PPBS," *Public Interest,* Summer 1967, p. 11.

8. Aaron Wildavsky, "The Political Economy of Efficiency: Cost Benefit Analysis, System Analysis, and Program Budgeting," *Public Administration Review*, 26 (1966), p. 303.

9. A. Wildavsky, *op. cit.*

10. See William M. Capron, "The Impact of Analysis on Bargaining in Government." A paper originally delivered at the 1966 Annual Meeting of the American Political Science Association; reprinted in James W. Davis Jr. (ed.), *Politics, Programs, and Budgets* (Englewood Cliffs, N.J.: Prentice-Hall, Inc., 1969).

11. Aaron Wildavsky, *The Politics of the Budgetary Process* (Boston: Little, Brown & Co., 1964).

12. Quoted in Richard F. Fenno, Jr., *The Power of the Purse* (Boston: Little, Brown & Co., 1966), p. 283.

13. *Ibid.*, p. 284.

14. *Ibid.*, p. 293.

15. *Ibid.*, p. 293.

16. *Ibid.*, p. 294.

17. *Ibid.*, p. 298.

18. *Ibid.*, p. 301.

19. A. Wildavsky, *op. cit.*, p. 51.

20. See W. M. Capron, *op. cit.*

★★★★
★★★★
THE POLITICS OF
ORGANIZATION

$\mathbf{T}$HIS CHAPTER deals with the structure of Executive
Branch organizations and describes conflicts that may
arise in this area. It discusses the significance of structural questions and points out some conditions that may
lead to demands for reorganization. The conditions under which reorganizations may be carried out are also
considered, as are the costs and obstacles to reorganization.

The Importance of Organization Structure

The behavioral revolution in political science and
public administration has unfortunately obscured the im-

Notes for this chapter appear on pages 210–211.

portance of an organization's formal structure. In the attempt to discover what lies beneath the surface, the surface has been ignored. Evidence to support this statement can be found by looking at the changing concerns of scholars in public administration and political science over the course of the last few decades. During the 1920s and 1930s they were often concerned with the "proper" forms of government and were often bent on improving everything from municipal administration to the national government. Political scientists headed boards and commissions of all sorts and made numerous recommendations. But after World War II this sort of activity began to decline and is rare now. Certainly the front-runners in the profession of political science are not often engaged in recommending changes in the structure of the government as a whole or in the structure of particular agencies.

Some of the apparent lack of concern for structure can be traced to the desire to appear value-free; one can scarcely make recommendations and appear value-free at the same time. Some can probably be traced to the increasing attention given the informal organization, and some can probably be traced to a declining interest in problems not immediately amenable to "behavioral" or quantitative study. The unconcern with structure is understandable and the attention to informal organization laudable, but ignoring the formal structure of organizations means ignoring an important area of bureaucratic conflict.

One does not need to be involved in making recommendations to recognize that many participants in bureaucratic politics are likely to engage in strenuous conflict to get the kind of structure they want. It could of course be possible that conflicts over structure are about nothing, that formal structure is meaningless. This view might make sense if conflicts over organization were few and far between, but they are not. They occur about as often as a reorganization is proposed. Because they occur so often, it seems reasonable to assume that structure is important, at least to the participants immediately involved. Why?

The formal allocation of power, of rights and responsibilities, of authorizations and limitations is effected by the structure of an organization. Indeed, to organize means to allocate power and responsibility and to reorganize means to change the existing pattern of allocation. Why may there be conflicts over organization and reorganization? Power is involved. Certainly, just who exercises power may have little to do with who has what powers on paper, even at the Presidential level. Political history is full of references to strong Presidents and weak Presidents. But even though there have been weak or ineffective Presidents, no one would argue that the formal powers of the President are meaningless. Formal powers give the man who has them an advantage in seeking actual power. They provide stepping stones to actual power.

Whenever a reorganization is proposed an important question is: What will this do to the organizational or program balance of power? Who will gain power? Who will lose? With answers, we are on our way to knowing who will favor the reorganization and who will oppose it. It may pay to be skeptical of statements maintaining that power relationships will not be affected. Such is the argument of those who stand to gain.

There are other reasons that may be given for the importance of formal organization, though all of them may be related to the basic question of power allocation. A formal organization chart is obviously something of a communications diagram; it shows who communicates with whom or, more politically, who has access to whom. Few would argue that all the communication within an organization is shown on the organization chart, but what the chart shows may be important —if only for symbolic reasons. One group may want its favorite governmental organization given cabinet status because that symbolizes access to the President and Presidential interest; another group may want its particular organization to be located in the Executive Office of the President for the same reason. By the same token an organization or group may resist being moved, if it means being cut off from the President or the department secretary. Bureaus within a department may resist being included in an administration or other subdepartmental organization headed by an Assistant Secretary if it might result in their losing direct contact with the Secretary.

Organization structure is important for other reasons. Who will be responsible for what is determined in some measure by the formal organization. This matter may be critical, because who is carrying out an activity may have an effect on what is done and how well. In other words, structure can affect program. What kind of water-pollution control program will be carried out by the federal government may be affected by the location of the program—in the Department of Health, Education, and Welfare or in the Department of the Interior. The programs and performance of the United States Forest Service are surely affected by its location in the United States Department of Agriculture. If it were located in Interior, a department to which users of public land have more access, its policies would almost surely be different. It can be noted that the Forest Service has steadfastly resisted being transferred to Interior.

The formal structure of an organization determines not only which units will be responsible but also which individuals. By reorganizing, shuffling responsibilities, and in some cases by moving someone to one side or "kicking him upstairs" the performance of an organization may change.

There is no need to dwell longer on the importance of organization structure. Organization structure is often the subject of intense political conflict as differently affected parties struggle for advantage, struggle to preserve and enhance their positions.

Why Are Reorganizations Proposed?

Granted that organizational structure is important and that proposals to change it will often occasion intense conflict, we can go on to ask why change proposals are made. Many of the answers were suggested in the last section. Proposals for reorganization may come from those who wish to increase their power, their visibility, their access to important decision-makers, or to alter the scope or emphasis of a particular program. But other conditions may also lead to reorganization proposals.[1]

As an organization increases in size it may reorganize; increasing size leads frequently to increasing specialization and increasing subdivision. As more and more people are added to an organization, more and more supervisory levels may be created. When an organization takes on more responsibilities, it must decide whether to give the new duties to an existing unit or to create a new one. When Congress authorizes a new program, it must decide whether to give responsibility for it to an existing organization or whether to create a new organization.

The growth of the Executive Branch testifies to the fact that new organizations are often created to administer new programs. The National Aeronautics and Space Administration did not exist until the United States had a space program, and the Atomic Energy Commission is an organization created to administer a new set of programs. Lest it be thought that the creation of such organizations is "obvious" or natural, it should be pointed out that an argument was made in both cases for lodging the space program and the atomic energy program in the hands of the military (the Department of Defense).

Related to changes in organization and program may be changes in workload. As the workload of an organization increases, more employees may have to be hired, and the increasing number of employees may make reorganization advisable. Alternatively, it may be possible to utilize an existing work force differently (reorganize) and thus cope with increased workload without taking on new employees. Workloads of course may decrease, and this too may affect organization structure.

Changes in work methods or technology may have an effect on organization structure. The most obvious example is the computer; its introduction may have a substantial effect on formal organization. Examples of the effects a computer can have are several: a clerical force may be much reduced in size, a staff of professional employees (programmers, mathematicians) may have to be employed; and decisions in the hands of middle management may be placed in the hands of top management. The introduction of machinery to replace men, automation, can have substantial effects on organization structure.

Demands for efficiency and economy may also lead to reorganization. One may well be skeptical here, because often there may be very little substantial evidence that reorganization will in fact lead to the claimed savings. The claim of efficiency and economy may be simply a rationalization for a reorganization intended to alter the distribution of power. Still one must admit that by centralizing purchasing, for example, it may be possible to buy at lower cost. Introducing machines and letting men go may lower production costs. Contracting jobs out instead of creating a government organization to do a job may keep costs lower. While efficiency and economy may be only surface goals of reorganization, they may also be the real goals.

Of course efficiency and economy are not the only covers for a politically motivated reorganization. All of the immediately foregoing justifications—changes in size, workload, program responsibilities, technology— may be used to justify a proposed reorganization that is intended to reallocate power or shift access, because they may seem relatively apolitical, or neutral, or technical. A neutral justification may be used in the hope that it will win more widespread support for a reorganization than a political justification would.

It should be kept in mind, of course, that even if a reorganization proposal results solely from a change in technology or size it still may have an effect (real or imagined) on the distribution of power and access and thus may be opposed by those who think they will be adversely affected. This observation leads to the most important point: that reorganization proposals are likely to have both multiple causes and multiple effects, though different participants will usually emphasize one effect or another.

The Sources of Reorganization Proposals

We have considered why reorganization proposals come up; we have not as yet considered the sources of reorganization proposals, but this subject is worth some attention as the source of a reorganization proposal may be related to its substance and its chances of success. We can begin by dividing the sources into two types— external and internal—and then look at each type more closely.

External sources are those outside the organization being reorganized, though not necessarily outside the government as a whole. There are a variety of such groups. Perhaps best known are the commissions and task forces appointed by the President to advise him either on general matters of government organization or on problems in a particular policy area, such as health, welfare, or defense. The two Hoover Commissions that inquired into the operations of the government in the late forties and early fifties are examples of this type of commission. The National Advisory Commission on Selective Service which made rather sweeping proposals for the reorganization of the Selective Service System is an example of a more specialized external body that makes recommendations.[2] In recent years a number of advisory commissions and task forces have been appointed—both publicly and on a confidential basis—and they have recommended changes in organization(s) administering the programs or coping with the problems they were set up to consider. Members of the White House Staff may make proposals for reorganization, as may the Bureau of the Budget and other central service and control agencies. A Secretary's office may propose changes in the bureau structure within the department. When we come to this level, though, we come close to internal sources of reorganization. But external-internal may be more of a continuum than a dichotomy.

The external sources named so far have all been more or less official sources. Even though many task forces and advisory commissions are composed largely if not exclusively of private citizens, they exist with official sanction. Suggestions for reorganization can come from the particular groups affected. Housing and urban groups for a long time asked for a Department of Urban Affairs, and finally the Housing and Home Finance Agency became the Department of Housing and Urban Development. Organized labor was delighted when it finally succeeded early in the twentieth century in getting a Department of Labor. Other groups or individuals with special interests have asked that particular departments or agencies be created to serve their interests or that a unit be created within the Executive Office of the President to look after a particular problem. Particular congressmen or committees may also suggest new organizations or the reorganization of existing ones.

What about internal sources of reorganization? It has been said already that departments may suggest and carry out reorganizations of their constituent bureaus. In addition, departments, agencies, and bureaus may initiate their own reorganizations, though in particular cases just who initiated what may not be clear. In 1966 the Department of the Navy reorganized itself, apparently on its own initiative.[3] After receiving a good deal of criticism the National Aeronautics and Space Administration began to examine carefully its own organization structure as well as its management processes, and it set up two new divisions.[4] In 1965 the Office of Education carried out a rather sweeping reorganization of itself.[5]

Principles, Proverbs, and Patterns

What forms are reorganization proposals likely to take? There is probably no branch or subject of administration where the supply of conventional wisdom is put to more use than in the field of organization design. And for good reason: there is very little sound research on the relationships between organization structure and organizational functioning. Usually, if not invariably, anything that might pass for data is lacking, and the proposers of reorganizations and new organizations rely on patterns and proverbs (often in the guise of principles), occasionally seasoned with a bit of imagination.[6]

Textbooks on public administration often mention purpose, process, area, and clientele and suggest that these words be borne in mind when considering the structure of an organization. Units with the same purpose should be grouped together, or units serving the same people, or units utilizing employees with the same skills. But what is not made clear is that it is usually impossible to say what is or ought to be the basis for any particular organization. Nor is it made clear that organization by purpose, process, area, and clientele may all be found in the same organization. To take only one example, the Selective Service System has an area organization (56 state headquarters and over 4,000 local boards), it has a specific purpose, and it has a specific clientele. If it were to be reorganized, would it make more sense to put it in the Department of Defense (it inducts men for military service), in the Department of Labor (it is obviously a manpower agency and collects data on men never inducted), or in the Veterans' Administration (so that the same agency could maintain files on men both before and after service.)? Conventional wisdom offers little assistance.

Conventional wisdom says that similar services should be grouped together (everything from secretarial pools to personnel recruiting to central purchasing to the government's education programs), but it is perfectly plain that in many circumstances the decentralization of services would be more flexible (and perhaps no more costly) than the centralization of services. Span of control is another common phrase; it means that the President or a Secretary or other executive can control only a limited number of subordinates and consequently should have only a limited number reporting to him. Put this way, it is sensible but hardly helpful. Put more specifically—that an executive can control no more than 10 or 15 or 20 or whatever subordinates—it is at best arguable and at worst nonsense. Everything depends on the ability of the executive, the ability of the subordinates, whether subordinates have limited discretion or unlimited, whether close supervision is a goal to be achieved or behavior to be avoided (a wide span of control makes close supervision impossible), whether subordinates are all doing the same thing or all doing separate things, and so on.

Clearly the common phrases, the proverbs, are little help. So patterns are commonly used. What does this mean? It means that organizational structures already in being are often copied when a new organization is created. And when existing structures are reorganized, they are reorganized along lines probably existing in another organization. In other words, the past experience of other organizations is copied. Now this does not mean there is systematic study of past experience, and certainly there is no systematic analysis of the effect of structure on performance. Rather there is simply copying with more or less modification based on personal experience, common sense, and conventional wisdom. All this is not to deny the existence of invention. Surely there is some, but there is more copying than inventing. Incrementalism reigns even more supreme in organization design than in budgeting. In the absence of substantial knowledge this may make sense. Still one is justified in being skeptical when a new organization or a reorganization is justified in terms of principle.

The Acceptance and Rejection of Reorganization Proposals

When are proposals for change likely to be made, and when are they likely to be accepted? A common time for changes to be proposed is when a new administration takes over, particularly when this involves a new party coming to power. Organization changes are likely to be part of the new program proposals of a new administration. If a new President presents a variety of new program proposals as did President Roosevelt, President Kennedy, and President Johnson, he is likely to present simultaneous proposals for new organizations to carry out his new programs or at least proposals for the restructuring of existing organizations.

Reorganization proposals are also likely when a particular program or existing structure becomes the subject of unusual criticism. In recent years, for example, such different organizations as the Post Office, the Secret

Service, and the Selective Service System have come under criticism for varying reasons; and reorganization proposals have in each case come on the heels of the criticism. Reorganization and improvement in performance are closely associated in the minds of both managers and politicians. Reorganization proposals are also likely whenever a manager finds that he is not getting what he wants and thinks a reorganization would be at least a partial solution (what he wants may be anything from more economical operation to faster decisions, more information, or increased control) or when a manager is faced with new demands that his existing structure cannot meet.

If half the question is, "When are reorganization proposals likely?" the other half is, "When will they be accepted?" More accurately perhaps the question is, "Under what conditions will proposals be accepted and under what conditions will they be rejected?" No hard and fast rules are possible; yet it does seem possible to suggest some conditions that if present will mean acceptance and if absent will mean rejection. They can most clearly be presented in the form of a list. A reorganization will be accepted if it has:

1. The President's support (acquiescence).
2. The Bureau of the Budget's support (acquiescence).
3. The support of top management in the immediately affected organization.
4. Support or acquiescence from other Executive Branch agencies.
5. Support or acquiescence from relevant committees in Senate and House.
6. Support or acquiescence from relevant interest groups.

There is little question that a reorganization proposal will be accepted if it has the support of all these groups; and many lower-level reorganizations do get ready acquiescence and can be thought of as routine reorganizations. Because many reorganization proposals do not have anything like unanimous support, their sources of support, the amount of influence the supporters have and how intensely they feel as opposed to the influence and intensity of the opponents are important. Some examples may clarify these points. The proposal of the National Advisory Commission on Selective Service to reorganize the Selective Service System fell flat. Why? The proposal came from a Presidential Commission, but was turned over by the President to another task force for further study. In other words, he did not immediately accept it, and furthermore he appointed the director of the Selective Service System to the task force. The director, General Hershey, was openly and consistently hostile to any reorganization, and allied with him were the chairmen of the House and Senate Armed Services Committees. Clearly with this kind of opposition and with the President apparently unwilling to press hard, the reorganization was bound to fail. The creation of the Department of Transportation presents the other side. There was opposition, both from affected agencies and from groups concerned, but the President wanted a Department of Transportation and was willing to work to get it. He compromised, he bargained, he persuaded—and the Department of Transportation was created.[7] There is no question that Presidential interest and influence were decisive. But it is also worth noting that the creation of the Department of Transportation had important symbols on its side. It was possible for supporters of the bill to point to the proposed new department and predict coordination, the elimination of waste and duplication, new efficiency and economy and rational planning.[8] Whether all these would result and in what degree was of course open to question, but that these favorable symbols could be associated with the reorganization was a plus.

These points suggest that successful reorganization proposals must appear to have commonly desirable goals, and of course the specific proposals must appear to lead to these goals. There would be little point in saying that elimination of overlap was a goal, if it were impossible to suggest how the reorganization would reach the goal.

The Costs of Reorganization

So far in our discussion of organization and reorganization we have mentioned only goals and hoped-for results; we have not mentioned the costs of reorganization. But these exist and can be great; so important are they that in inquiring into the acceptability of reorganization proposals it is worthwhile to consider the costs. What are they?

Depending on the type and extent of the reorganization, individuals may lose status, money, the chance for promotion, perhaps even their jobs. They may be required to learn new jobs or may have to behave in different ways. They may have to work with different people. At the organizational level there are also costs. Some employees may resign.[9] Morale may deteriorate. Access to higher levels of authority may change, and a new congressional committee may assume jurisdiction. New standards of performance may be expected. If units themselves are transferred from the parent organization and no new ones take their place, the parent organization obviously shrinks in size and budget and may shrink in prestige as well.

Both individuals and organizations may resist reorganization. For anyone affected to support a reorganization the benefits must appear to him to be greater than the costs; if they appear otherwise, he may be passive or hostile. It would be simple to say that for a change proposal to be accepted there must be more supporters than opposers, but this would be too simple. Intensity of feeling is important; a few intense individuals may be able to equal or overcome many men with relatively mild feelings. Political influence is also important. Many bureaucrats in opposition may not kill a proposal if the President favors it. Who opposes and supports is as important perhaps as how many support and oppose. But even here it is well to keep in mind the notion of cost-benefit. Even though he might have won the battle, the President perhaps did not fight for the Selective Service Reorganization because it might have cost him support in the Armed Services Committees—support he needed for measures that he considered more important.

These sections, like the preceding ones, have emphasized the politics of reorganization, with good reason. Structure, along with budgets, personnel, and program, may be a subject of political contention; and what structure emerges from a conflict may have implications for the balance of political power as well as for program effectiveness and administrative economy and efficiency. Surely not all reorganizations are hotly disputed, but then neither are all budget decisions. The potential for conflict is still there. *The Politics of the Budgetary Process* is a book that has been written; *The Politics of Reorganization* is a book that deserves to be.

Notes for Chapter 8

1. This discussion draws on an essay by Frederick C. Mosher, "Some Notes on Reorganizations in Public Agencies," in Roscoe C. Martin (ed.), *Public Administration and Democracy* (Syracuse: Syracuse University Press, 1965), pp. 129–150. See also Mosher's lengthy analysis in his *Governmental Reorganization: Cases and Commentary* (Indianapolis: Bobbs Merrill Co., 1967), pp. 475–537.

2. See *In Pursuit of Equity: Who Serves When Not All Serve*, Report of the National Advisory Commission on Selective Service (Washington: U.S.G.P.O., 1967). The reorganization suggested in this report was not carried out. Another example of reorganization proposals coming from an outside commission is provided by the commission appointed to investigate the assassination of President Kennedy. According to the *New York Times*, a reorganization of the Secret Service carried out in 1965 was "the direct result of the Warren Commission's investigation of the assassination of President Kennedy. The commission found several deficiencies in the service. . . ." *New York Times*, November 11, 1965.

3. See *The New York Times*, March 8, 1966, p. 1. "Secretary of the Navy Paul H. Nitze announced today a sweeping reorganization of the Navy's management structure. The principal changes will strengthen the authority of the Chief of Naval Operations and eliminate all but two of the traditional bureaus that once were virtually autonomous."

4. See the *New York Times,* April 5, 1967, p. 1. "With an eye to improving its operations, the National Aeronautics and Space Administration has begun a permanent, high-level review of its organization and management. . . . The operation began without fanfare last month with the creation of a new division to act as a sort of watchdog for the agency's headquarters in Washington and its 14 field centers, laboratories and launching bases. A new office for co-ordinating planning was also established."

5. See Stephen K. Bailey, "The Office of Education: The Politics of Rapid Growth," paper prepared for delivery at the 1966 Annual Meeting of the American Political Science Association, New York City.

6. A classic statement is Herbert Simon's "The Proverbs of Administration," *Public Administration Review* (Winter 1946), pp. 53–67.

7. The *New York Times* (March 13, 1966) reported that the Administration was optimistic over passage of the bill to create the Department of Transportation. "One reason for the optimism is that a deliberate attempt has been made to keep the bill as non-controversial as possible. . . . A key part of this strategy was to drop an attempt to establish uniform standards for setting rates, fares, route awards, and subsidies in different areas of transportation.'

8. See the testimony of administration officials in *Creating a Department of Transportation,* Hearings Before a Subcommittee of the Committee on Government Operations, House of Representatives, 89th Congress, 2nd session (Washington: U.S.G.P.O., 1966).

9. The *New York Times* (April 24, 1966) reported, "An exodus of administrative, scientific, and technical personnel, resulting from a governmental reorganization, is threatening to slow down President's Johnson's efforts to clean up the nation's water supplies."

CONCLUSION:
WHAT WE DON'T KNOW

IT MAY BE worthwhile to end this brief description of the Executive Branch with some mention of what is not known about it. What are the areas of ignorance? What are the subjects for research?

1. Not a great deal is known about problem-solving or program-development in Executive Branch agencies. In the Age of the Executive this may come as something of a surprise, but it is true nonetheless. An observation made by Stephen Bailey in 1966 is accurate: "In the continuum of Federal policy making, the Congress has received the lion's share of scholarly attention. The Supreme Court and the Presidency have not been ignored, but the explicators of their respective policy roles and of their institutional dynamics have been few —even if distinguished. Virtually ignored in Political

Science literature has been the policy role and the institutional behavior of the Federal department, agency, office or bureau."[1] We ought to know more than we do about the nature of the problem-finding and refinement process, about the generation of alternative programs/actions/solutions, about the analysis and evaluation process, and finally about the choice process.

2. Not a great deal is known, though more is becoming known, about the impact and effectiveness of government programs. Who is affected how? Who gets what? Are the programs having the effect that was initially intended? These questions often are not asked. Though we know better, the assumption seems to be that passage by Congress is what counts, and after that implementation is automatic. This of course is nonsense. Passage by Congress is just a beginning, and measuring the effectiveness of government programs (are they working and how well?) is an important area for research. Asking what particular government organizations are doing and how well they are doing it is also important.

3. What is the relationship between knowledge and policy? This is a general way of raising several important issues. Do the programs government agencies carry out reflect currently available knowledge? Are currently available techniques used to collect relevant information? As more information becomes available are programs adjusted accordingly? What are the obstacles to collecting information? What are the obstacles in the way of using it? How do organizations treat data that contradicts their programs and assumptions? These are only some of the questions that might be asked in this general area of research.

4. We know very little about particular government organizations as actors in the policy-making proc-

ess. Specifically, we know little about the variety of executive agency-congressional committee relations or the variety of executive agency-Presidential relations. There are a few case studies and a supply of convenient examples, but not much more. The relations between political and career officials (or Presidential and permanent officials) is also an area little-studied.

5. Little is known about either the partisan or the policy consequences of different kinds of administrative structures. In recent years a good deal of attention has been focused on grass-roots democracy and community participation, but there has been little systematic study of the consequences of community participation in the administration of federal programs. More attention might also be given to the consequences of government-contracting and grant-giving.

6. Coordination is a favorite word in the vocabulary of administration, but the mechanisms of coordination have not received much systematic attention; nor do we know much about the consequences of inadequate coordination, whatever that may mean. With a particular focus on program linkages, overlaps, and gaps it would be interesting to inquire into the performances of inter-agency committees, the central control agencies, the White House, Congressional committees, interest groups, and professional associations. What is being done by everyone, each unaware that anyone else is doing it? What is not getting done, because everyone thinks someone else is doing it?

7. We know that PPBS has spread (with varying success) throughout the Executive Branch. Other administrative practices have also spread. Studying the diffusion of administrative innovations might open up an interesting area in comparative administration and comparative organization theory.

8. For all the interest that public opinion studies have attracted in recent years, little attention has been given to public information and attitudes about government agencies and their programs. Lack of such public opinion research is one of the glaring gaps in the public administration literature, to say nothing of the general literature on American politics. How accurately do government programs reflect public opinion? With only a few exceptions, we do not know. It would also be interesting to study the attitudes of government officials toward their organizations, their programs, and their environment.

9. More research might be done on government agency secrecy and publicity to bring what we know up to date. The images that agencies try to build of themselves would be interesting to study and might well be joined with studies of the images that people have of them. The image-building activities themselves are worth study, and it would be interesting to see how the images of particular organizations vary throughout the bureaucracy and indeed the population as a whole.

10. Not much is known about the activities of lobbyists in the Executive Branch. Although lobbying activities in administrative agencies may be at least as important as such activities on Capitol Hill they have been much less studied. As lobbyists not active on Capitol Hill are not required to register, the data on administrative lobbying is sparse indeed. Yet it would be interesting to know more about lobbyists in the Executive Branch. What about their numbers, their access, their tactics, their success? And what do bureaucrats think about administrative lobbying?

11. The whole subject of administrative organization-clientele relations is worth more study than it has received. Starting first with the observation that many

organizations have a variety of clienteles and different organizations have different types of clienteles (compare a welfare agency and a police or penal agency), it would be interesting to study the variety of relationships that exist and the variety of images clienteles have of their organizations. The part that clienteles play in pointing out problems, suggesting actions, and providing support in the White House and in Congress is especially interesting.

Doubtless many other suggestions could be made, but these are enough to show that our ignorance of the Executive Branch is extensive. Substantial research is in order. What kind of research? Virtually any kind. There is room for historical studies of organizations, case studies of particular problems or decisions, and systematic surveys of attitudes. Both the devotee of documents and the devotee of questionnaires and interviews can find satisfaction in the Executive Branch. Much of the research can be simply descriptive. Description (mere description, it is commonly called) is frowned on today, but accurate description can be valuable. Before we can evaluate or modify our theories and models we need data, information, observation. The scientific enterprise requires description quite as much as abstraction. In addition to description, explanation and prediction are the common goals of research and may be the goals of research in the Executive Branch, though they need not be the goals of every particular study.

Some few studies by some daring souls might have prescription and improvement as their goals. Reaction to the principles of administration carried us too far; now professional political scientists are loathe to suggest any changes at all in the bureaucracy. But surely the lack of immutable principles does not mean there are no alternatives to the status quo. What are the alternatives? Might any of them be better than the status quo, or is the status quo as good as can be? Research might throw light on these questions, and they are worth lighting up.

In the end I would argue for research focused on particular organizations and programs. It is possible to study the Supreme Court as a whole and maybe even the Congress. But the Executive Branch is just too big. Studies in it must be fairly limited; and many studies are needed.

Note for Conclusion

1. Stephen K. Bailey, "The Office of Education: The Politics of Rapid Growth," Paper prepared for delivery at the 1966 Annual Meeting of the American Political Science Association, New York City, p. 1.

INDEX